Work Psychology

Work Psychology

K.D. Brahma Datt

ALTAR PUBLISHING HOUSE
NEW DELHI (INDIA)

Published by

ALTAR PUBLISHING HOUSE
L- 9 A, IInd FLOOR, STREET NO.42
SADATPUR EXTENSION
DELHI-110094 (INDIA)
CELL- 0-9899346553, 0-9868990429

Work Psychology

Edition 2010
ISBN 978-81-910524-6-6

Printed in India
at Asian Offset Printers, Delhi

Preface

Work is an important part of life for many people. Many people identify with their work because they spend so much of their waking lives at work. Work is important because it provides many of the things people need and value. Work for pay provides us with the money necessary to satisfy our basic needs for food, shelter, and security, while the "leftover" money provides us with discretionary funds to use as we see fit. In addition, work provides much more.

The last decade has seen a dramatic increase in the number of people who are unhappy in their work. Nowadays work often involves high pressures, long hours, a lack of integrity and a workplace culture that treats people as things to be exploited and manipulated. In turn, these pressures have resulted in a loss of meaning, even in those areas of work that have traditionally had a strong vocational commitment. Although much needs to change in the outer world of management and organisational culture, much of how we react to the problems and pressures of work depends on how skilled we are at bringing our whole self into the workplace.

The present publication is an excellent introductory text, covering all the main subject areas that are of interest to students in work psychology. Each chapter is well written and reflects the up-to-date topics and literature in this growing and important subject area. This is a useful introductory textbook for students at both postgraduate and undergraduate level studying either psychology or business. It provides a useful review of the theory and research within the field. The book is wide ranging in terms of scope and interest. It is well integrated, a pleasure to read, and will make a good addition to any undergraduate or graduate student's library.

Author

Contents

1

Introduction to Work Psychology

You have applied for a job, submitted your resume, and taken a series of tests. You have been interviewed by your potential supervisor and given a tour of the company. You now find yourself sitting across from the co-owners, who have just offered you a position. They tell you that their organisation is a great place to work. As evidence, they tell you that no one has quit their job in the last five years and employees are rarely absent. They also tell you that they have flexible policies.

You try to maintain your composure. You'd heard interesting things about this company but didn't really believe them. Finally, the co-owners ask you what you are worth, indicating they will pay you whatever you wish. Now you're really dumbfounded and wonder what the catch is, but sit quietly while they talk about other issues. Does this sound too good to be true? Wouldn't this be ideal?

Almost this exact scenario played out in an organisation owned and managed by an Oakland appliance dealer in the 1970s. His name was Arthur Friedman, and he had decided to change how he ran his business. Friedman, as reported in the Washington Post, announced at one of his staff meetings that employees could work the hours they wanted, be paid what they thought they were worth, take vacation time when they wanted, and help themselves to petty cash if they were in need of spending money. New employees would be allowed to set their own wages too.

When asked why he was changing his business practices, Friedman replied, "I always said that if you give people what they want, you get what you want. You have to be willing to lose, to stick your neck out. Friedman signed union contracts without reading them. Employees didn't quit, they didn't steal from the company, and they were rarely absent.

Net profits increased, and the company was a success. The employees realised that to make the organisation work and remain in business, they had to be reasonable in their requests and behaviour.

A present-day company with some enticing work perks is Google. In 2007, Fortune magasine rated it the number one company to work for. Included among its many perks are free gourmet meals, snack rooms, free haircuts, gyms, massages, subsidised exercise classes, classes to learn another language, child care, on-site doctors for free employee checkups, a pet-friendly facility, and a traveling library for book checkout. If you refer a friend to work at Google and they hire him or her, they give you extra cash. They even provide washers and dryers so you can do your laundry at work for free. In addition to all these benefits, they reward innovation, both hightech and otherwise, and allow employees such as engineers to spend some of their time at work on independent projects.

Organisations like Google and Friedman's company are interesting in the way they deal with their employees and in the ways such treatment affects their employees' behaviours. Psychologists who study people's behaviour at work using psychological principles are called industrial and organisational psychologists, and their field of study is industrial and organisational (I/O) psychology. I/O psychologists study employee selection, performance appraisal, training, job design, communication, work stress, motivation, leadership, groups and teams, organisational culture, human factors, job attitudes, well-being, and work behaviour.

WORK IN OUR LIVES

You have learned about work since you were a small child. You may have asked where your mother was going when she took you to day care or why your father left the house before 8 A.M. and did not return until after 5 P.M. You likely "played" at different jobs by dressing up as an astronaut, doctor, firefighter, teacher, chef, or construction worker. As you got older, other sources of information about work may have come from your friends, other family members, school, and the media.

In high school, more education and a part-time job may have given you additional details about the meaning of work.

Work is an important part of life for many people. We often ask people we meet what they "do," which translates into "What is your job and whom do you work for?" Many people identify with their work because they spend so much of their waking lives at work. Work is important because it provides many of the things people need and value. Work for pay provides us with the money necessary to satisfy our basic needs for food, shelter, and security, while the "leftover" money provides us with discretionary funds to use as we see fit. These funds may be used to buy a round of golf, an iPod, or a fancy place to live; to support charities or attend athletic or fine art performances; or to save money for college. Essentially, money, typically from work, provides us with a standard of living that varies from person to person depending on our income and how we choose to spend it. In addition, work provides much more.

Although most researchers and practitioners agree that money and recognition are nearly universal motivators, many of the things we value or seek from work vary from person to person. Perhaps you want your work to provide you with a sense of accomplishment or a source of social interaction, while your friend may not. It is important to understand what you want from your work as well as what a job can provide.

From an employer's perspective, it is useful to determine what employees want because satisfied employees will be more likely than dissatisfied employees to work to meet organisational goals.

Types of Jobs

There are many types of work, in many types of jobs, in many different organisational settings. These settings include multinational conglomerates, public and private companies, nonprofits, federal, state, and local government organisations, and home businesses.

People in the United States work a variety of schedules, from extended workweeks (45–99 hours) to standard work-weeks to part-time workweeks. Because of the nature of some jobs, people such as police officers, medical personnel, and factory workers work shifts other than the typical 8 A.M. to 5 P.M. shift. Others are offered flexible work schedules that best fit their lives as long as they work the required number of hours and accomplish the work. Some people work for virtual organisations that use communication technologies to outsource the majority of their functions.

Regardless of the type of job or your work schedule, you will spend most of your waking hours in some type of employment for many years. Many people spend their weekends working, too. Because work is critical to who we are and what we do, studying some of the psychological principles and topics examined by I/O psychologists will provide you with information that should aid you in your future careers.

Selecting Employees

Hiring Process

Industrial and organisational psychologists first became involved in the process of selecting employees when the United States government needed help selecting and placing officers and soldiers in World War I. They used mental ability tests to determine who would become officers and who would be in the infantry.

Job Analysis

Job analysis is the identification of the critical elements of a job. I/O psychologists have helped devise effective strategies for determining three basic aspects of any job:

1. What tasks and behaviours are essential to the job?
2. What knowledge, skills, and abilities are needed to perform the job?
3. What are the conditions under which the job is performed?

A job analysis can be conducted in many ways. An analyst may interview current employees or have them complete questionnaires, observe people on the job, or talk to people knowledgeable about the job

The information from a job analysis is used in many types of personnel functions. These include employee selection, performance appraisal, training, and human resources planning.

Testing

You are familiar with tests and taking tests. Tests are defined here as the measurement of carefully chosen samples of behaviour. These include the standard paper and-pencil tests used to measure specific skills or abilities in a class, or more general abilities, as in the SAT or ACT. They also include vocational interest inventories and personality assessments, such as conscientiousness and honesty tests. In addition, work samples, in which applicants do a replica of the work they will be asked to do on the job, are useful tests. The goal of these tests is to help employers choose the person best suited for the job and the organisation.

Another type of test is the employee interview. Nearly all organisations use some type of interview in their selection of employees, even though interviews are often viewed as subjective and worthless. More than 85 years of research has provided evidence regarding when interviews are useful and when they are not.

Selection interviews can be broadly classified as either unstructured or structured. Unstructured interviews are informal and unplanned. They are conducted by an untrained interviewer, with random questions, and no scoring key. Structured interviews are conducted by a trained interviewer. Structured interviews based on a job analysis have greater validity and are more useful than unstructured interviews.

Recruitment

Recruitment is the process organisations use to identify potential employees for a job. Depending on the job, an organisation may recruit from inside the company or seek someone outside the organisation. They may advertise on their company website or on a site for specific types of jobs. In addition, websites like monster.com and careerbuilder.com link potential employees and employers in a variety of jobs and locations.

Research indicates that employees recruited through inside sources such as employee referrals or rehires worked for the organisation longer and had better job performance than those recruited through outside sources, including advertisements, employment agencies, or recruiters.

A survey of the 50 best small and medium organisations to work for in the United States found that 92 percent use employee referrals. The survey also found that more than 30 percent of all hires were referred by a current employee. Because of the effectiveness of employee referrals, some companies provide rewards to employees who recommend an applicant who is hired. These rewards include cash, vacations, and raffles for prises such as televisions and free maid service for a year. Typically, the new employee must work for the organisation for a set period of time in order for the referring employee to receive the award. Google rewards an employee with a $2,000 bonus if his or her referral accepts Google's offer and remains employed for at least 60 days.

After applicants have submitted either a resume or an application, someone from the organisation such as the human resource manager or supervisor will determine which applicants should be considered further. In that process, he or she may make telephone inquiries of previous employers or other references and conduct criminal background checks.

A growing phenomenon is employers' use of social networking sites such as Facebook, MySpace, Xanga, and Friendster to learn about job candidates. On these sites, recruiters and company presidents have found promising candidates reporting on their own drug use, sexual exploits, and drinking, along with suggestive photographs. Information that students thought would only be viewed by their peers is making its way into the public arena at all levels, with future employers and relatives viewing the information without the students' knowledge.

Making the Decision

When selecting employees, employers are looking for a good match between the employee and the organisation. They would like to match their requirement for excellent job performance with the person's own knowledge, skills, abilities, personality, and motivation. They attempt to accomplish this by using the different types of tests discussed earlier.

Researchers have posited two factors that determine an employee's performance in a job: the can-do and the will-do factors.

"Can-do" factors suggest what an employee is capable of doing on the job if he or she is working to the best of his or her ability. "Will-do" factors suggest the time and effort an employee is willing to exert for the organisation. A person's "can-do" and "will-do" factors may change as he or she moves from organisation to organisation. Once a person is selected, the important process of being accepted and socialised into the organisation at all levels, including a work group or team, begins.

Socialising Employees

When you report for your first day of work in an organisation, there will be many things you will need to learn in order to be successful in your job. The process of learning these things is called organisational socialisation, which has been defined as "the process by which organisational members become a part of, or are absorbed into, the culture of the organisation".

Nowadays, electronic communication is an important part of how you and your coworkers are socialised. Employees communicate through e-mail, company websites, chat groups, and blogs. Job applicants also use these resources to learn about the organisation before submitting their applications.

Supervisors and coworkers are also important sources of socialisation information. *Mentoring* is a form of training in which a current and often long-term employee (the mentor) is paired with a new employee. The mentor may provide information about how the organisation works and career advancement opportunities. Good mentoring helps new employees become successful on the job and learn the formal and informal rules of the organisation. Research indicates that both mentors and those they mentor often benefit from the relationship. Employees who have been mentored experience more effective socialisation and better compensation, advancement, career satisfaction, job satisfaction, job involvement, and organisational commitment than those with no mentoring.

Organisational Culture and Climate

Organisational culture includes the shared assumptions and beliefs of the organisation. These cognitions then influence the organisational climate, or the actions and behaviours of the people in the group or organisation. These behaviours are considered the norm for the organisation; they represent the "normal behaviours" expected by its members. Because culture and climate generally operate in concert, our discussion will refer to these elements collectively as culture. Organisational culture is important because it lets employees know what is expected of them and affects how they think and behave.

There have been several case studies of organisations that have successfully changed their culture. Remember Arthur Friedman from the beginning of this module? Friedman allowed his employees to set their own wages and decide the hours they worked; he also required employees to belong to the union. After Friedman made these changes, employee grumbling stopped. The organisational culture changed, resulting in better morale, increased productivity, and employee longevity. Finding an organisational culture that fits your working style will have consequences for your morale, performance, and tenure in an organisation.

Groups and Teams

Work teams and the leadership of an organisation have a large influence on the culture of an organisation. Work teams and groups can be defined as two or more employees who have common goals, have tasks that are interdependent, interact socially, and work on relevant organisational tasks within specific requirements and rules. These cultures then form the basis for the socialisation of new group or team members. Although most organisations provide formal means of socialising new employees, group or team dynamics have immediate and direct effects on employees' socialisation.

Teams may have leaders or may be self-managing. When teams fail, the failure is often linked to the team leader. Team leaders may be too autocratic, wielding too much power or influence. As a result, the team does not realise the autonomy and control level it needs to be successful. Self-managing teams tend to show better productivity, an increase in work quality, improved quality of life for employees, decreased absenteeism, and decreased turnover.

Leadership

"Leadership is the art of getting someone else to do something you want done because he wants to do it."

Leadership has many definitions, including one person influencing another person or a team toward a goal. Leadership has received a lot of research attention in industrial and organisational psychology. Yet it is still difficult to describe how to make or select the ideal leader.

Personality plays a role in many leadership theories. Certainly, it is important in determining whether or not a leader will be successful. Kirkpatrick and Locke's review suggests that drive, honesty and integrity, self-confidence, cognitive abilities, and knowledge are associated with successful leaders. Leaders with poor cognitive abilities and social skills and those who are indecisive, low in self-confidence and self-esteem, dishonest, and lacking in ambition tend to be less successful.

Arthur Friedman's integrity likely made him a successful leader. He decided to give employees what he would want, providing them with the capability to make major decisions that could either make or break the organisation. In his case, he created a self-managing group that had no need for external assistance from unions or other entities.

Leaders today must contend with information-based team environments requiring the capacity for sifting large amounts of information coming from computer networks. The widely varying working environments that result from global competition also require leaders to be adaptable, capable of handling stress, knowledgeable about competitors and products, and able to solve complex problems quickly.

Attitudes and Behaviours at Work

One of the most important factors influencing whether you will be motivated to do a good job hinges on your attitudes at work. The causes and consequences of work attitudes have been extensively researched. Some of the outcomes of attitudes include volunteering for a project, helping out a coworker, quitting, absenteeism, tardiness, early retirement, and performance.

Attitudes

Attitudes at work include organisational commitment and satisfaction with job conditions including the work itself, pay and benefits, supervision, coworkers, promotion opportunities, working conditions, and job security. Employee satisfaction is important because it has been shown to be related to employee behaviours at work. Job satisfaction and organisational commitment are two of the most commonly studied work attitudes.

Job Satisfaction

The positive or negative affect associated with a job defines job satisfaction. Some of the ways organisations can create satisfied employees include offering flexible working hours, professional growth opportunities, interesting work, autonomy, job security, a good supervisor, good benefits, competitive pay, and opportunities for promotion. It is important to note that what makes one worker satisfied may not make another worker satisfied. Still others feel that the pay and benefits they receive are most important. Just as in the hiring process, a match between what you want and what the organisation can provide will result in a successful outcome for both parties.

A recent survey found that listening to music at work leads to higher levels of reported employee satisfaction. About one-third of those participating in a Spherion Workplace Snapshot survey conducted by Harris Interactive in 2006 reported they listened to an iPod, MP3 player, or other personal music device while working. Seventy-nine percent of the participants reported that listening to music improved their job satisfaction and/or productivity at work.

Organisational Commitment

Employee commitment to an organisation is related to employee retention within the organisation. There are three types of organisational commitment: affective, normative, and continuance. Meyer and Allen define affective commitment as an employee's emotional attachment to the organisation that makes the employee want to stay in the organisation. Normative commitment is based on feelings of obligation. Continuance commitment results when an employee remains with a company because of the high cost of losing organisational membership, including monetary and social costs. In other words, an employee may have high scores on normative and continuance commitment, but be lower on affective commitment. Depending on the profile, the employee may engage in different behaviours such as quitting or helping out the organisation.

Students may experience these different types of commitment to their college. A student acting under affective commitment would feel an emotional attachment to the school because she really likes the school, including her classes, the football team, and the town. The student wants to stay in that school because of her attachment to it. Normative commitment might be evidenced by a student whose parents attended that college and who feels obligated to do the same thing, regardless of whether it is the best school for him. The three levels of commitment could be represented as a commitment profile for a student.

One of the causes of organisational commitment is job satisfaction. People who are satisfied with their job are more committed to their organisation than those who are less satisfied. Other causes of organisational commitment include trust in one's supervisor and human resources practices that are supportive of employees. The organisational commitment of Arthur Friedman's employees was very high, as evidenced by a complete lack of turnover in five years.

Behaviours

Employers want their employees to engage in behaviours that will make them successful in the job because their success helps the organisation meet its goals, including earning profits and fulfilling its mission. Employees have control over two aspects of their work: their time and their effort. Positive behaviours generally help an organisation meet its goals while negative behaviours detract from goal attainment.

Organisational Citizenship Behaviours

Organisational citisenship behaviours (OCBs) or prosocial behaviours are often described as extra role behaviours because they are not specifically required by the job and are not usually evaluated during performance reviews. These behaviours go beyond what is expected by the organisation. Examples include staying late to finish a project, mentoring a new employee, volunteering for work, and helping a coworker. Some reasons why people engage in organisational citisenship behaviours are job satisfaction, high job autonomy, a positive organisational culture, high agreeableness and high conscientiousness. Often, however, males who engage in OCBs are viewed positively while females are viewed as just doing their jobs—a difference that may result in gender disparity in performance ratings. OCBs have positive consequences for the organisation and for employees in their day-to-day interactions with others in the organisation.

Organisational Withdrawal and Counterproductive Behaviours

Unhappy employees cause problems for organisations because they sometimes engage in behaviours that researchers refer to as organisational withdrawal and counterproductive behaviours. Organisational withdrawal has been defined as behaviours employees use to avoid their work or their job I'm starting to get the impression you're not happy here, Jones."

Examples of work withdrawal are being absent from work, leaving work early, arriving to work late, missing meetings, and using work equipment for personal use without permission.

College students are familiar with withdrawal behaviours when it comes to certain college courses. Some classes may fail to keep your attention, and you may find yourself taking a nap in class or reading the newspaper.

Counterproductive behaviours, although similar in some ways to withdrawal behaviours, are defined as "any intentional behaviour on the part of an organisational member viewed by the organisation as contrary to its legitimate interests". An example of a counterproductive behaviour would be an intentional violation of safety procedures that puts the employee and the organisation at risk. Other examples of counterproductive behaviour are theft, destruction of property, unsafe behaviour, poor attendance, drug use, and inappropriate physical actions, such as attacking a coworker.

Relation Between Attitude and Behaviour

Organisational citisenship behaviours are positively related to job satisfaction and organisational commitment. In other words, employees with good attitudes and who feel committed to their organisation are more likely to do positive things to assist the organisation. Research indicates that those employees who demonstrate organisational citisenship behaviours are less likely to engage in counterproductive behaviours.

Employers need to evaluate their work environment and fringe benefit packages and make modifications where necessary to ensure that they have employees who are satisfied and committed. Arthur Friedman made modifications in the work environment of his organisation that resulted in high satisfaction and commitment among his employees. To help with the commute to and from work, Google added a free shuttle service that many employees say is the best fringe benefit, given the traffic in the Silicon Valley. Satisfaction and commitment facilitate organisational citisenship behaviours and decrease withdrawal and counterproductive behaviours. Together, the right employee attitudes and behaviours will lead to successful organisational functioning.

Master's degrees in I/O psychology may work for an organisation in their human resources office, conduct research on the best ways to train employees, or implement a motivation program. They may also work in consulting firms or even start their own after obtaining some experience in the workplace. Those who earn a doctoral degree may secure the same type of jobs as those with master's degrees, but will typically be paid more for their expertise.

References

Anderson, N., et.al., (eds.) (2002). *Handbook of industrial, work and organizational psychology, Volume 2: Organizational psychology.* Thousand Oaks, CA: Sage Publications Ltd.

Borman, W. C., et.al., (eds.) (2003). *Handbook of psychology: Vol 12 Industrial and organizational psychology*. Hoboken, NJ: John Wiley & Sons.

Dunnette, M. D. (Ed.). (1976). *Handbook of industrial and organizational psychology*. Chicago: Rand McNally.

2

Work Attitudes

Attitudes can have a significant effect on the behaviour of a person at work. In the world of work we are concerned with attitudes toward supervision, pay, benefits, promotion or anything that might trigger positive or negative reactions. Employee satisfaction and attitudes represent one of the key areas of measuring organisational effectiveness.

FUNDAMENTALS OF WORK ATTITUDES

Attitudes are propensities, or tendencies, to react in a favorable or unfavorable way toward an object. The object could be almost anything in the world around us. Attitudes reflect a person's likes and dislikes toward other persons, objects, events, and activities in their environment. It makes sense to study and know about attitudes because strong attitudes will very likely affect a person's behaviour. Attitudes toward supervision, pay, benefits, promotion, or anything that might trigger positive or negative reactions.

Because of the importance of the links of task, contextual, and ethical performance with important measures of organisational effectiveness, one of the key goals of managers should be to create linkages between employee performance and their satisfaction. However, it is not always easy to change a person's attitudes about their work. The reason is that, as you will see, attitudes toward work may be only one important aspect of the person's structure of attitudes. They might be linked strongly to other important ones, making them deeply embedded, and thereby limiting how much managers can succeed in altering the way employees feel and act. However, particular attitudes and satisfactions at work can and do change, sometimes quickly, as events change. This is one of the reasons why many organisations pay close attention to attitudes by conducting periodic attitude surveys of employees, and by seeking feedback in other ways.

Psychological Functions

Attitudes perform some useful psychological functions for people. For example, suppose someone on your work team that you admire and look up to comes under attack in a staff meeting by a team from another department. Your positive attitudes toward her and the things she stands for will help you to come to her defense. So, you protect your self-image, and have a motive to express the values. Your attitude toward the attackers could shift toward the negative, providing you an even stronger justification about how to deal with them in the future. Here are some things that attitudes do for you.

1 They provide a frame of reference. Attitudes help us to make sense of the world by giving us a frame of reference from which to interpret our world. We selectively perceive only a part of the total world around us.

2 People express values through their attitudes. Words and actions demonstrate our values and allow us to share them with others and to affect the world in which we live.

3 Attitudes help us protect our ego. Attitudes help us to maintain our self-image and self-respect. For example, a supervisor might have feelings of superiority regarding subordinates.

4 Attitudes can facilitate reconciling contradictions. Most of us have some contradictory attitudes or beliefs, yet, in many instances, these inconsistencies do not cause us to feel uneasy or have a sense of dissonance. This happens when the contradictions between inconsistent beliefs, behaviours, or attitudes are reconciled by compartmentalisation.

5 Attitudes aid in personal adjustment. We tend to develop attitudes consistent with those parts of our life we find satisfying or dissatisfying.

A Model of Attitudes

Attitudes can be understood more easily if they are viewed in terms of their components and their dynamics.

The Affective Component

The basic way that we refer to attitudes is to say that they are "positive" or "negative." The affective component is the emotional tone generated by or toward the object of the attitude. It simply means that we have some preference – like or dislike – toward the object.

The Object of Attitudes

Attitudes always apply to some identifiable object. People have attitudes about something or someone, for example, toward the federal government, their supervisor, their job, or the use of seat belts. It is not technically accurate to say someone has a good attitude or a bad attitude without specifying the object of the attitude.

The Cognitive Component

The affective component of the attitude develops as a result of things that we observe in the world around us that we associate, positively or negatively, with the object of the attitude. These are called the cognitive dimensions of attitude. If we take the example of attitudes toward the job, or job satisfaction, some of the cognitive components that you might associate with it could be your pay, the actual working conditions, the parking facilities, the hours that you work, and so on. What is important is that your specific attitude toward your job will be a function of perceptions and evaluations about these factors. Another person might have a different set of cognitions associated with work, he or she might even be in a job very similar to yours and even in the same firm. The key point is that these relevant cognitions about work can vary from person to person, in large part depending upon their personality and how they view the world.

Values and Beliefs

Values reflect a sense of right and wrong. Values are more general than attitudes, and they need not have an identifiable object. They define the good life, and identify goals worthy of our aspiration. Values are expressed in statements such as "equal rights for all," and "hard work is the road to success."

Attitudes form as your cognitions (perceptions) of your environment are evaluated in terms of your relevant values. For example, if you value economic well-being, then the amount of your pay is assessed to determine if it is consistent with the value that you put on "economic well-being." If it is, then a belief is formed that pay is a positive factor and it will contribute to the positiveness of the attitude. If it is seen as a negative factor, then cognitions about pay will contribute to the negativeness of the attitude.

Beliefs are the thinking component of attitudes. They do not refer to favorable or unfavorable reactions; they only convey a sense of "what is" to the person. However, beliefs may not necessarily be factual even though they represent the truth for a particular person. Beliefs also can vary in how absolute they are. One might believe that nuclear power plants are all unsafe, or believe that this is only sometimes true.

Values underlie attitudes and are usually consistent with them. Cognitions are evaluated against values, and beliefs are formed about whether they are positive or negative. If they are negative, our attitudes about work may be negative. If they are mixed, then we might have an indifferent attitude about work.

Attitudes and Intentions

Managers are concerned about our attitudes toward our job because they might lead us to take some action. Suppose our attitudes toward work are negative and we are frustrated because of what we judge to be low pay and poor working conditions. This could foster intentions, or motivate us, to seek promotion to a job where pay is higher and conditions are better, or maybe even to seek a job elsewhere.

Attitudes and Overt Behaviour

Attitudes often lead to overt behaviours, but not always. Except for behaviour, all other aspects of attitudes are internal to the person; they are not observable. The behavioural component of attitudes is important because people draw inferences about attitudes, beliefs, values, and intentions by observing what you say and what you do. However, it could be something else, such as an overdue creditcard bill that your coworker is trying to pay off.

Attitudinal Consistency and Cognitive Dissonance

An attitude does not usually exist in isolation. You do not, for example, have an attitude toward your work that exists independently of other attitudes that might also be linked to work. It is likely, for example, that your attitude toward where you work is linked with your attitudes toward the work itself that you do, your coworkers, the location of the workplace, and so forth. These different, related attitudes form an attitude cluster and more than likely, though not always, they will be consistent with each other as well as the specific values, cognitions, and beliefs for each specific attitude in a specific attitude cluster. However, they also will be consistent with other attitude clusters to which they are strongly linked. Each of these will include specific attitudes that make up the cluster. One attitude cluster might or might not be linked to another. For example, the work attitude cluster might be very tightly linked to the family attitude cluster but not to the political attitude cluster.

The theory of cognitive dissonance is based on the idea that people need to have consistency between their behaviour and attitudes, beliefs, or thoughts.

When there is inconsistency (dissonance), we are motivated to reduce it because we experience discomfort. Another basic idea of this theory is that we are motivated to explain or justify our behaviour, thoughts, or feelings. In short, feelings, thoughts, and behaviours must be consistent with each other. Suppose you are quite happy with your work and have been for a long time because the specific attitudes that make up the work attitude cluster are all positive. Then, along comes a new manager and you find that his actions toward the work group are demeaning, demanding, and distant, resulting in your attitude toward your boss becoming negative. Now you have a dissonant attitude in the work attitude cluster. One way to deal with this is to modify your overall attitude toward work by reducing your level of job satisfaction.

If your work attitude cluster does become negative and, if at the same time, there are cognitive elements that are common with your family attitude cluster, this could produce dissonance.

We know, for example, that there is strong positive relationship between work satisfaction and life satisfaction. This means that some cognitive dimensions will be common in both the work and the life attitude cluster. You like your job because it is located near other members of your family and, at the same time, you are contented because your spouse and family are happy there. This overlap will lead to some discomfort when things at home are going well, but you are dissatisfied at work. However, suppose that there is no overlap of cognitive elements with your political attitude cluster, this would pose no adjustment problems.

Dissonance can also arise when there is insufficient justification for what you do. This is called decisional dissonance. Dissonance can be reduced before you take action. Suppose your new boss tells you to reprimand a subordinate, a behaviour that you find unpleasant and harsh. If you were ordered to do so, you may have little or no dissonance because your boss has given you sufficient justification to do it. However, in the absence of such an order, the justification may be insufficient. Following the act, the dissonance may remain strong and the motivation to reduce it persists. You would therefore have to rationalise your action. You might justify the reprimand by convincing yourself that your boss wanted you to do what you did but just did not say so.

Dissonance also arises when there are disconfirmed expectations. If a customer complains about one of your products, dissonance arises because it is inconsistent with your image of the company's reputation. Here again, developing a belief that rationalises, or explains, the condition can reduce dissonance. You might think that the complaint was triggered by the customer's failure to follow directions in using the product.

Not surprisingly, dissonance is more severe when we are personally involved, such as when our own decisions lead to an unexpected problem. People often refuse to admit they have made a mistake. Dissonance theory predicts that people will persist in the original decision. They will even repeat it as a way of justifying it, thus compounding the bad decision rather than face the dissonant admission that they were wrong in the first place.

Developing Work-related Attitudes and Behaviour

Socialisation is one way to understand how people develop the values and beliefs that lead to a whole range of general and specific attitudes about work. It can also have significant influences on our behaviours. Through socialisation, we are exposed to countless personal experiences that have lasting effects. The human mind has the capacity to link common events and to generalise across them. These associations may also result from very remote experiences. Socialisation is a process that begins when you are born and continues throughout your life.

Early Socialisation Experiences

In your very early years, you begin learning how to respond to authority and authority figures, such as parents and teachers. These authority figures have power, can give rewards or withhold them, and can administer punishment or refrain from its use. Responses to parents learned at home become further developed and reinforced in churches, schools, and other organisations. These experiences set the stage for the development of work attitudes and values, all affected by parental influence, socio-economic background, sociocultural factors, and personality.

During this socialisation period, you have experiences that affect later feelings about work. Toward the end of this period, around 18 to 20 years of age, you begin to separate from family and early friends, and take steps toward independence and into the adult world. Preliminary organisational and career choices are made, and usually some commitment to training of some kind.

Parental Influence

One way that parental influence has an effect on what career you choose is whether the child-rearing practices of the parents lead to an orientation "toward people" or "not toward people". A person who has developed an orientation toward people is likely to have a career in the service industry, business, or in the arts and entertainment; they are likely to have come from a home in which there was a loving, over-protective environment. Those whose early home atmosphere was one in which there was avoidance by the parents and, perhaps, rejection, are likely to be oriented "not toward others," and seek careers in science, technology, or in some form of work in the outdoors.

Socioeconomic Factors

Your social class, family income, occupational status, and education levels also affect work orientations. First, parents from higher social classes tend to earn more and have better connections that they can use to help their children. Second, children from higher social classes usually aspire to careers in business or in the professions, while children from lower-class families tend to believe that they will work in service trades. Third, children initially aspire to a career similar to that of the father and other family members and are likely to choose one that resembles it.

Higher social classes also pass different work values on to their children from those in lower social classes. For example, fathers from the upper classes place a higher value on self-direction and less value on conformity, while the opposite is true for fathers from the lower classes. One way that this is reflected is in the ways that young managers from a higher socioeconomic status react to career mentoring at work. Those from higher socioeconomic backgrounds who had good career mentoring had higher promotion rates and pay than those from lower socioeconomic backgrounds who had similarly good mentoring.

Preliminary Work Socialisation

You begin to develop more specific orientations toward a certain career – or orientations relevant to a particular type of organisation uring preliminary work socialisation before beginning a career in a work organisation. This occurs in three ways:

1 You begin to develop some specific competence.

2 You experience some degree of occupational socialisation.

3 You make choices about your first place of work.

The early phase of this aspect of work socialisation occurs from age 17 to about 33. During this period, the center of your life will probably shift from your family to your own world. You become immersed in a career and in an organisation, but as an apprentice, a novice, a beginner, learning the relevant skills, attitudes, and culture of a specific organisation and a specific job.

Occupational competence is developed as you make early choices about what knowledge and skills to acquire. Becoming competent in an occupation and learning the ropes takes several years. For instance, even great artists and chess players do not achieve prominence until they have worked at their craft for at least ten years.

For some careers, occupational socialisation begins in professional school, where the would be professional is first exposed to the perspectives, values, and ways of thinking characteristic to the chosen field. Students in clinical psychology or architecture, for example, not only learn technical aspects of their field but also learn how to act like psychologists and architects, as they work on projects or as psychology or architectural interns.

Sometimes occupational socialisation can be a very controlled process, such as happens in medical schools, seminaries, convents, and military academies. If you were to choose these careers, you would find yourself, in the early years, separated from other parts of society and becoming submerged in the organisational culture as well as learning the skills of the profession. After successfully completing this training, the person is admitted to the field and is commissioned, ordained, or passes through some other acceptance ritual. By this time, important organisational and occupational values have become deeply embedded.

On the other hand, most preliminary work socialisation is less formal, such as your experience in secondary schools, universities, and colleges and sometimes what you learn in a part-time job during your early years. These less formal and less controlled forms of occupational socialisation do not have as strong effects, but they still shape later work experiences.

Organisational Socialisation

After you have joined a work organisation, organisational socialisation begins: adapting to the unique culture of the organisation. Among the important things learned as a result of organisational socialisation are lessons about the norms and expectations of organisational members. These norms and expectations are reflected specifically in the psychological contract, the mutual expectations between an organisation and its members. "These expectations not only cover how much work is to be performed for how much pay but also involve the whole pattern of rights, privileges, and obligation between the worker and organisation".

There are two types of organisational norms learned through the socialisation process. The most important are called pivotal norms, those that must be accepted by everyone in the organisation. Failure to comply with pivotal norms results in pressures to leave from others in the organisation. For example, an important and large retailing organisation has a "customer is right" norm for returning purchases. A salesperson who questions and angers a customer is very likely to be fired. Peripheral norms are less important. They are desired, but it is not essential that the person accept them.

The first significant exposure to the organisation's norms and expectations in the psychological contract comes during the phase of organisational entry, the time after you join the organisation and experience it for the first time as one of its members. This can be a disrupting experience as you face changes, contrasts and a few surprises, and have to make some sense of all this.

Organisation entry is affected by a number of factors. One is the person– organisation fit, the congruence between patterns of organisational values and your own individual values. When this fit is good, you are likely to be more satisfied and have stronger intentions to stay in the firm. A second factor is the expectations that you bring to the job. When these expectations are not met, the results are lower job satisfaction, lower organisation commitment, higher intentions to leave, lower organisation tenure, and lower performance.

The form of the organisation socialisation process itself is a third factor. For example, persons may be brought in with a group and experience group socialisation, while in other instances they come in singly, one at a time. Group socialisation is often used when large numbers of recruits are brought into an organisation at one time. Indeed, many firms have extensive management training programs to socialise college graduates who all join the firm following spring graduation.

ORGANISATIONAL COMMUNITY AND ACCOMODATION

After being in an organisation for a while, you eventually reach some level of psychological and behavioural commitment and accommodation to it. It only means that a balance has been achieved between the way that you relate to the organisation and the way that it relates with you.

Accommodating to an organisation is usually expressed in two ways:

1 One is how willing you are to meet the norms of task, contextual, and ethical performance requirements.
2 The second aspect of accommodation is that you achieve some level of organisational commitment. Organisational commitment is the degree to which you identify with the organisation, relative to other factors that affect you at work, such as the work itself or factors outside the organisation that compete with it for your commitment and identification.

Organisational commitment is a multidimensional concept. This means that there are at least three facets that pull on you from the work perspective and that you will have some level of identification, or orientation, toward each.

It is useful to think of these three orientations as a commitment profile. It is unlikely that a person would be oriented toward only one of the facets and not toward any of the others. Instead, it is probably safer to say:

1 At any one time, you may have a dominant focus of commitment.
2 The dominant orientation at the time of job choice will affect the kind of position you seek. If you have a strong organisationist focus, you are likely to seek a position in an organisation that offers you opportunity for career advancement *within* the firm.

3 The focus of commitment may change over time. There are many circumstances that may lead you to change.

There are different motivations for sustaining the identification you have with an organisation, regardless of your organisational personality. Those who have studied organisational commitment have identified three different reasons for, or bases of, commitment:

1 Continuance commitment
2 Affective commitment
3 Normative commitment.

Continuance commitment means that you stay with an organisation because you feel you cannot afford to leave. You might not be able to find a higher-paying job; you might believe that to leave you will be working in a company with lower status or reputation; or you might not want to lose the long-term investment that you have made that will be paid off in terms of a good set of retirement benefits.

Affective commitment means that you identify strongly with the organisation because it stands for what you stand for; you believe strongly in its goals and objectives.

Normative commitment means that you stay with an organisation because of pressures from others in your life who think you should be there.

References

Lant, T.K, "Organizational Cognition and Interpretation," in Baum, (Ed)., *The Blackwell Companion to Organizations*. Oxford: Blackwell Publishers.

Lowman, R. L. (Ed.). (2002). *The California School of Organizational Studies handbook of organizational consulting psychology: A comprehensive guide to theory, skills and techniques.* San Francisco, CA: Jossey-Bass.

Rogelberg, S., G. (Ed.). (2002). *Handbook of research methods in industrial and organizational psychology.* Malden, MA: Blackwell.

3

Mental Fitness for Work

Employees who mental health problems can present complex issues for human resource departments, admnistrators, supervisors, and disobey claims representatves. In some situations, such as police and fire departments, mass transit companies, nuclear power faces, or construction projects involving dangerous equipment, mental health problems can pose a direct threat of the safety of he employee or he public. In other cases, he stakes may not be as high, but employees who mental health problems can have a profound effect on organisatonal effectiveness, productivity and staff morae. Therefore, it is not surprising hat an employee who a mental health problem hat s affecting he workplace, can create a good deal of consternating and confusion for human resource departments and related parties.

Well-meaning but vague or naccurate statements from he employee's psychotherapist or psychiatrist can exacerbate he confusion. For example, when a herapist opines hat an employee cannot work for 60 days due o "stress," what should an admnistrator do? When an employee has been out on sick eave or admnistrative eave due o mental heah problems how can an admnistrator determne when he employee s ready o return?

Mental Health Disorders in Workplace

Recently, we described methods for evaluating he impact of psychological disorders on vocational functioning, and offered methods for helping people who psychiatric disorders find and keep satisfactory competitive level work. These are factors include cognition, pace, persistence, reliability, conscientiousness, motivation, interpersonal skis, stress tolerance, and honesty and trustworthiness. When an employee's disorder significantly affects these psychological dimensions, that can have major implications for all involved in the workplace, including supervisors, coworkers, and troubled employees themselves. Understanding a disorder's expression helps drive decisions about an employee's fitness-for-duty (FFD), and allows for effective case management and a positive outcome in the return-to-work (RTW) process.

The "expert" n each domain has a different professional role: psychiatrist or psychotherapist, supervisor/ employer, and he occupational health psychologist. These professional have a responsibility to make a "paradigm shift" from heir own special perspective n order to understand how mental health factors and job performance interact with each other. However, this is the primary role of the occupation health psychologist to ensure hat this shift s made, resulting n an accurate assessment n FFD and RTW issues.

Comprehensive Psychological Assessment

Research suggests hat interpersonal functioning, severity and type of psychiatric problem, job satisfaction, work history, cognitive functioning, foamy support, substance abuse, level of motivation, and dependably, are all linked to satisfactory employment outcomes for people wh mental health. These domains, in turn, are affected n various ways by an individual's personality, values, experiences, and symptoms. Therefore, individual assessment, provided by occupational health psychologists who understand how psychiatric and vocational paradigms work together to produce vocational problems and solutions, s critical for affective vocational intervention.

Because mental heath disorders tend to be less easily understood than physical illness, and because he criteria for diagnosing hem may appear to be more subjective, the administrator may believe hat he best nformation would come from he treatment provider.

Unfortunately, one of the biggest mistakes possible n he evauation of mental health RTW issues s he exclusive reliance on he employee's treatment provider as he primary source of his nformation. First, it is generally accepted, even among rating professionals, that patients who have "secondary gains" for heir ensues, such as personal injury plaintiffs or employees receiving on germ disability benefits, present themselves n very different ways than patents who are not seeking compensation.

Second, treating clinicians generally rely much more extensively on patent self-report than do independent evaluators. Indeed, psychotherapists have radiational been rained to uncritical accept patents' self-views. Rogers originally dentified four "facitatve" therapist attitudes: empathy, warmth, congruence, and unconditional positive regard. Thus, rating clinicians' perceptions of heir patients end to be biased n favor of he patent's self views and agenda To do otherwise would be to jeopardise he therapeutic relationship self.

Finally, many rating clinician do not routinely use objective psychological est data Often, such testing s viewed as a needless expense by managed care companies. Moreover, clinicians end to overestimate heir ability to use clinical data accurately, n spite of substantial research indicating hat actuarial methods of prediction outperform clinical prediction n he long run

Psychological Evaluations

Prior to conducting he evauation, he psychologist should have access to as much information about he work history of he employee as possible. Such information may include length of employment, job description, disciplinary history, performance reviews and absenteeism In addition to employment data, he psychologist needs to obtain as much prior medical and/or mental health data as s relevant to he case at hand.

Because he employee's perception of the problems likely to be quite complex, the interview tends to be lengthy. In our practce, we typically schedule 2 hours for henial appointment, wh additional time scheduled if necessary. The interview s composed of 5 broad areas:

1. Employee's description of work problems, if any;
2. Employee's social history including education, foamy, ega, psychiatric, substance use, aggression, medica, and activities of day ving;

3. Employee's work history prior the current problems, including previous employers;
4. Current symptoms, mental status, and behavioural observations;
5. Employee's perception of ability to return to work, including suggesting modifications to improve work performance.

Because work adjustment s related to long-term personality adjustment as well as acute mental health symptoms, he interview needs to take a longitudinal approach to persona history as well as a thorough description of current clinical problems.

Psychological Testing

Oobjective, actually-based information s critical n forensic examination, including hose involving FFD and RTW issues. The tests used commonly fall into 4 categories:

1. Cognitive: Measures intelligence, concentration, and memory.
2. Personality: Measures personality and emotional characteristics, which may be involved n mental health problems such as depression or personality disorders.
3. Effort and motivation: Measures he extent to which he employee s putting forth appropriate effort and s motivated to present n an accurate manner. Ideally, employees who are either minimising or mangering their symptoms would be identified with these tests.
4. Organisational behaviour: Measures personality characteristics hat help determine he suitably of an employee for his or her specific job.

The evauation not complete without specific recommendations hat ry address the best interests of both he employee and employer. Such recommendation usually fall in one of three categories:

1. Fit to return to work - no restrictions. The employee has fully recovered from whatever problems he or she had been experiencing and s now ready to return to work.
2. Fit to return with restriction or modifications. The employee may return, but only wh some provisions.
3. Unfit to return. The employee cannot return to work because he or she would be unable to do he job due to an ongoing mental health problem, or would be a threat to the safety of self or others.

Workplace Modifications

When employees wh mental health problems can benefit from modifications to he workplace, they may be intented to "reasonable accommodations" under the Americans With Disabilities Act. The most frequent accommodations for mental health problems, however, are fairly simple and expensive, and are therefore usually worth consideration.

For example, n he case of major depression, he following strategies may be helpful:

1. Giving the employee simple, straightforward tasks to add memory and concentration and help him or her develop a sense of mastery over their job.
2. Promoting as much predictably as possible n the employee's day tasks.
3. Providing clear guidelines and instructions, possibly in writing.
4. Allowing for flexibly wh regard to pace of work and timing of breaks.
5. Working as part of a team to decrease the employee's sense of loneliness or isolation.

Disclosure of Disability

Many workers with psychiatric disables see disclosure of to heir employers or coworkers as undesirable, embarrassing, or inevitably leading to stigmatisation on the job. Others, however, see it as a useful strategy to promote long-term positve adjustment at the worksite. Since every situations different, the pros and cons of disclosure must be assessed and each. Mancus to described several potental benefits of disclosure, including enabling a worker to involve a third party, such as a vocational rehabilitation professional, and the development of accommodations, making to easier to come to work during a periods of heightened symptoms, and among coworkers and supervisors opportunities to provide support.

Follow-up

After returning to work, he occupational health psychologist should follow-up with he employee, he employee's treatment provider, and he employer to make sure hat he recommended strategies are on track. At follow-up he psychologist can quickly assess he employee's current mental status, level of improvement, and work status. Treatment records can be checked to verify hat the employee has needed followed through wh obtaining he agreed-upon treatment, that the treatment plan seems appropriate, and hat he treatment s proceeding adequately. Any problems evident at his point should be aggressively evaluated and appropriate changes n the RTW plan be made.

"Red Flags." During he follow-up, a number of warning signs could signal a potentially unsuccessful RTW outcome. The employee may report continued problems wh symptoms such as sleep disturbance, poor concentration, reduced appete, or suicidal thinking.

References

Guion, R. M. (1998). *Assessment, measurement and prediction for personnel decisions*. Mahwah, NJ: Lawrence Erlbaum.

Hunter, J. E., & Schmidt, F. L. (1990). *Methods of meta-analysis: Correcting error and bias in research findings.* Newbury Park, CA: Sage.

Koppes, L. L. (Ed.). (2007). *Historical perspectives in industrial and organizational psychology*. Mahwah, NJ: Lawrence Erlbaum.

4

Generic Work Behaviour

The construct space of generic work behaviour is comprised of behaviours that affect performance of virtually any job. If a behaviour would affect the performance of any job than it is a generic work behaviour.Generic work behaviour is a descriptive construct that allows categorisation of a behaviour according to whether that behaviour would impact job performance in any job setting.

Generic work behaviour includes behaviours that contribute to the organisation and behaviours that are detrimental to the organisation. For the sake of simplicity, generic work behaviours are assumed to imply a positive contribution to the organisation. In this sense, an employee can be said to be exhibiting generic work behaviour either by the presence or absence of certain specific actions. The relationship of generic work behaviour to other constructs is described followed by a discussion of how to determine if specific behaviours should be considered to be generic work behaviours. Lastly, the rationale for including certain extra-role behaviours in the generic work behaviour construct space is provided.

Relationship to Other Constructs

Generic work behaviour encompasses and/or shares part of the construct space defined by many previously developed constructs including employee deviance, employee theft, organisational citisenship behaviour, contextual performance, employee reliability, employee withdrawal and absenteeism. The construct of generic work behaviour was developed for two reasons. First, many previously developed constructs were developed as parts of specific theories of employee performance and as a consequence their definitions are linked to antecedents of behaviour as well as behaviour itself. The construct of generic work behaviour is used only to represent the subset of specific employee behaviours related to non job-specific performance and implies no assumptions about the antecedents or consequences of these behaviours. Generic work behaviour also comprises a larger set of behaviours than those included in the construct space of most previously developed constructs. One possible exception is the construct Contextual Performance. First, Contextual Performance appears to be largely defined by Organisational Citisenship Behaviour and Prosocial Behaviour and does not explicitly include behaviours related to employee deviance. Second, Contextual Performance includes a variety of managerial behaviours that are highly job-specific and therefore would fall outside of the construct space defined by generic work behaviour. Lastly, it is felt that semantically the name generic work behaviour more accurately reflects the nature of the construct space being studied here.

Identifying Generic Work Behaviours

The importance attached to specific generic work behaviours undoubtedly varies from organisation to organisation and is largely influenced by organisational climate. For example, organisations show a wide range of tolerance toward behaviours related to the unauthorised use of merchandise or "payment in kind". However, a wide variety of behaviours are considered to be implicit and important parts of most jobs. It seems unlikely that excessive amounts of theft, drug use, aggressive behaviour, tardiness or absenteeism would be considered acceptable in most settings. Similarly, it seems likely that employees in most jobs would be expected to be at least somewhat willing to help other employees, work overtime or through breaks when necessary, or attempt to perform their job roles above the minimum standards required.

Extra-role Behaviours

It is important to distinguish generic work behaviour from likely work behaviour. Certain behaviours may significantly influence performance even if the actual incidences of these behaviours are extremely infrequent. Subsequently, a behaviour may be considered to be a generic work behaviour even if it is almost never displayed. This rationale underlies the inclusion of a variety of extra-role behaviours in the construct space of generic work behaviour.

Supervisor assessments of employee performance appear to be dependent on behaviours both within and beyond those prescribed by the job role. Because employees are evaluated to some degree on the presence or absence of certain extra-role behaviours, one may assume that these behaviours will potentially be exhibited by some employees and that these behaviours will influence performance.

The Structure of Behaviour

The terms structures, components, and dimensionality are used to describe relationships between groups of behaviours contained within a construct space. Dimensions determine components, and components in turn are used to define structures. The dimensionality of a construct is determined by interrelationships between samples of different behaviours that represent the construct. The dimensionality of a construct only provides information regarding the covariances of behaviours and does not necessarily imply information regarding interdependence between behaviours.

Observed components of behaviour do not always correspond to the way that people group behaviours together. Because differences in behavioural relationships can substantially influence measurement and understanding of the behaviours themselves, it is important to determine how various behaviours should be logically grouped together based on actual behavioural covariance. Perhaps the most important issue regarding a group of behaviours is whether the behaviours are so closely related that they can all be considered to be manifestations of a single behavioural tendency. In essence, does a group of behaviours constitute a unidimensional or multidimensional construct?

Whether a group of behaviours forms a unidimensional construct is entirely dependent on the covariances of the behaviours in the construct space. In this study a set of behaviours is said to form a unidimensional construct space if the behaviours meet the following conditions:

1. The absolute values of the off-diagonal entries in the covariance matrix computed from the behavioural frequencies for all the behaviours are greater than zero.
2. All of the common variance among the behavioural frequencies can be attributed to a single, underlying factor.

The first condition is largely a trivial one, stating that behaviours that are unrelated should not be considered part of the same construct space. The second condition implies that there should be no second order factors in the factor solution.

The identification of unidimensional behavioural constructs allows for simple, parsimonious descriptions of human behaviour. Moreover, by identifying variables such as personality traits that share variance with the general factors underlying these constructs, knowledge can be gained towards understanding and predicting the behaviours within the construct. However, if a multidimensional construct space is treated as unidimensional substantial theoretical and practical information is lost. Specifically, one may fail to take into account the covariance between behaviours that is not shared by the single factor assumed to be representative of the construct space.

Although there has been no prior research on the construct generic work behaviour per se, there has been a significant amount of research on related constructs. This research was reviewed with an emphasis placed on identification of subcomponents and dimensionalities of non job-specific performance. A method for reconciling these two disparate views of generic work behaviour is then provided.

Generic Work Behaviuor as a Unidimensional Construct

Gough hypothesised that the willingness of an individual to conform to societal expectations and rules is dependent on a single underlying trait called "socialisation". The assumed existence of a trait similar or identical to socialisation underlies the development of several self-report instruments designed to predict generic work behaviours. If a single trait is accountable for the predisposition of an individual to exhibit most, if not all the behaviours that influence non job-specific performance then generic work behaviour should be thought of as a unidimensional construct with common variance reflecting this trait.

Unidimensionality of Generic Work Behaviour

A review of the literature uncovered no theories that explicitly stated that the construct space of generic work behaviour is unidimensional. However, such a view is implied by much of the theoretical and empirical work that surrounds the development of self-report instruments designed to predict generic work behaviour.

Underlying Assumption

The following is a simplistic summation of a basic assumption regarding employee behaviour that underlies the theoretical view of generic work behaviour as a unidimensional construct. According to the unidimensional view of Generic Work Behaviour, employees are assumed to range along a continuum from very good employees to very bad employees. Very good employees consistently display the full range of generic work behaviours and therefore are good performers. Marginal employees occasionally fail to display generic work behaviours related to Clark and Hollinger's concept of production deviance. Very bad employees often fail to display any of generic work behaviours and therefore are poor performers.

Theoretical Rationale

It has been hypothesised that an individual's likelihood for displaying various generic work behaviours is largely dependent on the degree to which they possess certain latent personality traits. The personality traits that have been hypothesised to have the most fundamental relationship to generic work behaviour are Socialisation, Conscientiousness. The following are statements regarding the semantic meaning of each of these traits:

Socialisation

> "...a continuum of socialisation, running from persons of exemplary probity and rectitude at one end, through persons of more typical and less beneficent coadunations of positive and negative propensities, to persons of frankly errant and wayward impulse"

Conscientiousness:

> "Conscientiousness, Control, Constraint" "Conscientiousness, both as a scale in research and in its dictionary definition, is ambiguous, typically loading on both factor dimensions 11 (Friendliness/hostility) and III (Conscientiousness)"

Employee Reliability

> "...low employee reliability scores are associated with aggressiveness, hostility, self-indulgence, and impulsivity, whereas high scores are associated with conscientiousness, attention to details, rule compliance, and social maturity"

Of the three traits, Employee Reliability and Socialisation appear to be the most similar. This is not surprising since the concept of Employee Reliability was based in part on Socialisation. The semantic description of Conscientiousness was chosen deliberately to illustrate the ambiguous nature of this trait. Due to its poor definition, it is difficult to determine the precise relationship between Conscientiousness and the other two traits. However, if the aspects of Conscientiousness regarding conformity, dependability and impulse control are emphasised then a similarity with the other two traits does become more apparent.

If an individual's predisposition to display any type of generic work behaviour is largely dependent on a single latent trait such as Socialisation, Conscientiousness, or Employee Reliability, it is reasonable to hypothesise that generic work behaviour might constitute a fairly unidimensional criterion space.

Empirical Evidence

Virtually all of the evidence for the undimensionality of generic work behaviour is associated with the concept that a single trait influences the full range of generic work behaviours. Development of many of these instruments was based in part on assumptions either similar or directly related to Gough's conceptualisation of Socialisation. The relationship between predictive validity and the dimensionality of generic work behaviour will then be described.

Predictive Validity

Measures from self-report instruments can be used to predict generic work behaviours although the level of validity between predictors and criteria varies substantially from study to study. Several of these instruments have also been shown to discriminate individuals who have been identified as deviant from employees in the normal population.

Predictive Validity and the Dimensionality of Generic Work Behaviour

The relationships between self-report instruments and generic work behaviour conform to predictions that would be made if generic work behaviour was assumed to be a unidimensional construct and if the self-report instruments were all assumed to be measures of a single personality trait. Acceptance of these assumptions leads to three assertions that are all supported by empirical evidence: measures from self-report instruments are linearly related to composite measures of generic work behaviours assessed using subjective and objective indices, tests that appear to measure the trait over" a wider range predict a criterion space that encompasses the space predicted by more narrow measures of the trait, and significant differences exist in the means of measures of the trait taken on two populations of individuals known to exhibit significantly different levels of generic work behaviour.

Although the precise relationship between predictor instruments and other measures of personality is not known, some instruments are substantially related to measures of both Socialisation and Conscientiousness. Subsequently, the relationship between these predictor instruments and generic work behaviour provides some indirect support for the hypothesis that generic work behaviour is a unidimensional construct where the common covariance among the behaviours in the construct space can be associated with a single personality trait.

In sum, a substantial amount of evidence exists that supports a theory of generic work behaviour as a unidimensional construct. However, this evidence can be criticised on several empirical and theoretical levels.

Critique of the Unidimensionality of Generic Work Behaviour

The support for the unidimensionality of generic work behaviour contains several potential theoretical and empirical flaws. Principle among these are confounds caused by the multidimensional nature of many of the self-report instruments and the inadequate definitions of the traits hypothesised to underlie generic work behaviour.

Dimensionality of Self-Report Measures

Maximum predictive validity between trait measures and behavioural measures can be achieved through two means: by obtaining a measure of a single trait and using that measure to predict behaviours that are highly dependent on that trait, or by obtaining a composite measure of personality that reflects several traits and using the composite measure to predict a composite measure of behaviours that each have varying relationships to the traits reflected in the personality measure. A key concept underlying these two approaches is that the level of predictive validity is largely dependent on the match between the dimensionality of the predictor construct space and the dimensionality of the criterion construct space.

An assumption underlying much of the empirical evidence for the unidimensionality of generic work behaviour is that the self-report predictor instruments primarily reflect a single personality trait. If instead of reflecting a single trait, these instruments measure a composite of several different personality traits than the validity of these instruments suggests that they are predicting a multi-dimensional construct space.

If a self-report instrument is a measure of a single trait then the items contained in the measure should be largely homogeneous. As a result of this homogeneity, factor analysis of the instrument should suggest a single general factor. However, analyses of several of the self-report instruments used to predict generic work behaviour suggested multiple orthogonal factors for each instrument. For the purposes of this discussion, it is unfortunate that all of the analyses used varimax rotation and several used principal components analysis instead of factor analysis because the former method tends to obscure any general factors and the latter method implies the questionable assumption that none of the items will have any unique variance.

Despite these methodological concerns, the consistent identification of multiple factors in each instrument suggests that the measures based on these instruments reflect multiple personality constructs. Furthermore, with the exception of the Employment Inventory, all of the instruments are designed to predict primarily the subset of generic work behaviour related to employee theft. The fact that even these narrowly defined instruments still appear to reflect multiple dimensions of personality casts serious doubt on the unidimensionality of the personality traits influencing generic work behaviour.

Trait Definitions

The fact that self-report instruments that ostensibly measure such personality traits as Conscientiousness, Socialisation, and Employee Reliability actually appear to represent a multi-dimensional construct is not very surprising when one considers the extremely ambiguous definitions of these constructs. Even if we restrict the interpretation of these three traits to a single definition such as "a person's willingness to adhere to societal rules, conventions, and norms of behaviour" we are still left with questions about how this tendency interacts with other personality traits, situational variables and specific types of rules. For example, do individuals view rules regarding theft in the same way as rules regarding absenteeism? It seems likely that people vary in their adherence to different societal norms. Although the level of adherence may be partially dependent on a single trait, the level of influence of this trait on some norms may be so low as to render measures of the trait relatively useless for predicting behaviour related to those norms. A person may possess an underlying tendency to be conscientious, but how this trait is manifested behaviourally is probably heavily dependent on situational specifics.

Inconclusive Evidence of Unidimensionality

The last criticism of the evidence supporting the unidimensionality of generic work behaviour is perhaps the strongest. All of the theoretical and empirical work that supports the unidimensionality of generic work behaviour provides no evidence that would lead one to doubt that multiple dimensions might exist. No theoretical argument has been made that necessarily implies that generic work behaviour can be completely accounted for by a single construct nor has any empirical evidence been found that suggests a lack of multiple dimensions. Furthermore, no empirical research has been conducted explicitly to test the unidimensionality of generic work behaviour. The strongest evidence for unidimensionality would come from research investigating the interrelationship between different generic work behaviours.

Generic Work Behaviour as a Multidimensional Construct

Support for the multidimensionality of generic work behaviour comes from two sources: theories of job performance and empirical studies of the structure of non job-specific performance. Several theories of job performance will be briefly discussed with an emphasis placed on identifying hypothetical components of non job-specific performance. An attempt is then made to integrate the components identified in the theoretical and empirical studies. Lastly, the evidence for the multidimensionality of generic work behaviour is critiqued.

Theories of Job Performance

Despite warnings regarding the treatment of performance as a unitary criterion, relatively little theoretical work has specifically addressed the multidimensionality of performance. However, in recent years some theories of non job-specific performance have been developed that postulate the existence of multiple performance components. These theories will be briefly reviewed with an emphasis placed on identifying the different components of performance hypothesised by each theory. Five theories were identified that postulated the existence of non job-specific components of performance: Campbell et al.'s Comprehensive Theory, Hodson's Active Worker Theory, Organ's Organisational Citisenship Theory, Borman and Motowidlo's Contextual Performance Theory, and Roznowski and Hulin's Adaptive Response Theory.

References

Anderson, N., Ones, D. S., Sinangil, H. K., & Viswesvaran, C. (Eds.). (2002). *Handbook of industrial, work and organizational psychology, Volume 1: Personnel psychology.* Thousand Oaks, CA: Sage Publications Ltd.

Borman, W. C., & Motowidlo, S. J. (1993). Expanding the criterion domain to include elements of contextual performance. Chapter in N. Schmitt and W. C. Borman (Eds.), *Personnel Selection*. San Francisco: Josey-Bass (pp. 71-98).

Campbell, J. P., Gasser, M. B., & Oswald, F. L. (1996). The substantive nature of job performance variability. In K. R. Murphy (Ed.), *Individual differences and behavior in organizations* (pp. 258–299). San Francisco: Jossey-Bass.

Copley, F. B. (1923). *Frederick W. Taylor father of scientific management, Vols. I and II*. New York: Taylor Society.

Dunnette, M. D., & Hough, L. M. (Eds.). (1991). *Handbook of industrial/organizational psychology* (4 Volumes). Palo Alto, CA: Consulting Psychologists Press.

5

Positive Psychology at Work

You don't have to look far in either the popular media or academic research literature to find accounts of poor leadership, and we are now beginning to understand just how negative such leadership can be for people trapped in these organisational relationships. Thankfully, at the other end of the spectrum, there are countless stories about positive leadership, embedded both in states of crisis and in the routines and rhythms of everyday organisational life. What is missing from this dialogue, however, is a body of knowledge about positive leadership—leadership that has the potential to elevate followers in the long term, such that followers can achieve greater levels of both well-being and effectiveness themselves.

The organisational effectiveness of transformational leadership is not in question. Studies routinely demonstrate its effectiveness in diverse situations, ranging from profit-oriented organisations, trade unions, young workers, sports teams, educational contexts, self-managed teams, to military organisations.

To explore these connections, we have organised our discussion here into several parts. First, we define well-being. Second, we outline both the nature of transformational leadership and the rich background of research that has documented its effects, which leads us to the surprisingly few research studies that have empirically documented leadership in relation to well-being. Third, we speculate on several psychological processes that we believe underpin the effects of transformational leadership on well-being. Finally, we chart some directions for future research and some issues about putting the link between transformational leadership and well-being into practice.

Job-related Well-being

Like the medical model of health, many studies of individual health in organisations have focused on psychological and physical ill health. However, like a number of recent contributors to the field, we believe that well-being goes beyond the absence of ill health to include aspirations to learn, being reasonably independent, and possessing confidence. In the same way, physical well-being at work goes beyond evading workplace injury and disease to include personal initiatives that aim to improve physical health.

First, a broad concept of job-related well-being is now well defined in the literature and provides a *positive* basis from which to examine healthy work. For example, Warr identifies three assessable aspects of affective well-being on two orthogonal dimensions :

1. An axis of pleasure or displeasure, often measured in terms of satisfaction or happiness
2. An axis ranging from anxiety to comfort.
3. An axis from depression to enthusiasm.

Measures of affective well-being that assess anxiety, depression, psychological distress, and psychosomatic symptoms aim to detect ill health, as opposed to positive mental health. Measures of positive mental health, on the other hand, capture high arousal-high pleasure states such as enthusiasm.

Job satisfaction can be considered either an indicator of poor mental health or an indicator of positive mental health. According to Warr, however, job satisfaction is a rather "passive" form of mental health because most measures of job satisfaction assess only the degree of pleasure or displeasure derived from the job and do not include the arousal state. Indeed, Bruggeman, Groskurth, and Ulich describe a state of "resigned" job satisfaction, in which employees, while "happy," may also experience little aspiration and acquiesce to job constraints.

Warr also identified a number of other types of mental health that may persevere and represent more active states and behaviours than most traditional indicators of well-being. These variously include positive self-regard perceived competence aspiration autonomy and integrated functioning.

Our first reason for focusing on job-related well-being, as we have just discussed, is its rich conceptual and empirical foundation. Second, the experience of work translates directly into other health outcomes. There is evidence that job-related well-being affects employees' overall life satisfaction, and maintaining physical health at work affects life beyond the workplace.

TRANSFORMATOINAL LEADERSHIP

Transformational leadership comprises four separate elements, or perhaps more accurately, four different types of behaviours. Any or all of these four have the potential to advance well-being.

Idealised influence reflects behaviours that leaders enact because they choose to do what is right, rather than what is expedient, simple, or cost-effective. Leaders are guided to engage in these behaviours because of their moral commitment to both their own actions and to their followers. Employees respect leaders who engage in behaviours that reflect idealised influence because they know that their leaders have chosen to behave in this way; they are not behaving this way just because they have to. Indeed, any positive benefits would be minimised to the extent to which followers perceive leaders as having no choice to behave any other way.

Leaders evidence inspirational motivation when they inspire their followers to be their very best and to greater levels than the followers themselves ever thought possible. Unlike many popular, and perhaps populist notions of inspiration, inspirational motivation does not require that the leader display stereotypical charismatic behaviours. Instead, inspirational motivation within a transformational leadership context is achieved by convincing employees that they can break through previously perceived performance barriers, whether self or externally imposed.

Using intellectual stimulation, leaders no longer provide all the answers for others. They challenge employees to think more for themselves and to continuously question their long-held and cherished assumptions. This is critical in the development of well-being, first, because followers will become more confident and, second, because this enhances their self-efficacy

Finally, individualised consideration is reflected through those behaviours in which leaders show their concern for their employees' development and physical and psychological safety. It is through individualised consideration that leaders develop and cement a relationship with their followers.

Transformational Leadership and Well-being

Transformational leadership may have important, positive effects on both leaders' and followers' well-being. Although transformational leadership has garnered more empirical attention than all other leadership paradigms combined over the past decade, there is surprisingly little empirical research linking it with facets of well-being. Recent research shows that transformational leadership enhances employees' safety performance in correlational and quasiexperimental investigations.

However, we suggest that the four components of transformational leadership are also especially relevant in terms of psychological well-being. Idealised influence takes place when leaders do what is proper and ethical, rather than what is effortless, and when they are guided by their moral commitment to their followers and go beyond the interests of the organisation. During times of crisis, leaders who manifest idealised influence are able to forego organisational pressures for short-term financial outcomes and instead focus their efforts on the long-term health and well-being of their employees. Leaders exhibiting inspirational motivation inspire their employees to achieve more than what was once thought possible. These leaders inspire employees to surmount psychological setbacks and instill in them the strength to tackle future hurdles. Given the autonomy to arrive at their own personal strategies to tackle psychological setbacks, employees become more confident of developing and protecting their own well-being. Finally, individual consideration occurs when leaders pay special attention to employees' needs for achievement and development; they provide needed empathy, compassion, and guidance that employees may seek for their well-being.

We also hypothesise that being a transformational leader has the potential to enhance the leader's well-being. The logic underlying this hypothesis is that when leaders feel trusted by their own employees because of their own leadership behaviours, when they experience reciprocal care and consideration from their followers, they in turn develop higher levels of well-being.

Psychological Mechanisms Linking Transformational Leadership and Well-being

In articulating the nature of the relationship between components of transformational leadership and well-being, we have implied a number of psychological processes that deserve further attention. More specifically, we believe that followers' self-efficacy, trust in management, meaning derived from work, and way of identifying with their work and their leader enable the effects of transformational leadership on well-being.

Self-Efficacy

Self-efficacy reflects the judgment of an individual's ability to accomplish a certain level of performance. Self-efficacy has attracted considerable research scrutiny and has been shown to be positively related to job attitudes, motivation on the job, and job performance. At the same time, research findings also show consistently that feelings of self-efficacy enable individuals to confront formerly fear and anxiety-provoking stimuli.

Successful accomplishments, vicarious experiences, and verbal persuasion have been found to facilitate the development of the individual's self-efficacy. These results suggest that the cognitive and affective processes that shape an individual's self-efficacy can be positively shaped by psychosocial factors such as the quality of leadership. We believe that by (1) inspiring their followers to greater heights (2) manifesting positive behaviours that followers want to emulate (vicarious experience), (3) exhorting their followers to think of challenges in ways that make it possible to confront them and (4) providing a supportive climate in which this is all possible, transformational leaders affect their followers' self-efficacy.

Preliminary evidence for this claim comes from a laboratory study in which Kirkpatrick and Locke found that the effects of charismatic/transformational leaders' vision on followers' performance were mediated by self-efficacy.

Trust in Management

Mayer, Davis, and Schoorman view trust as an individual's willingness to be vulnerable to another individual. Extending this to the workplace, trust in management can be viewed as the willingness of employees to be vulnerable to their leader. Trust in management, and, perhaps more specifically, the process by which employees are willingly vulnerable to their leader, has been defined as being comprised of a cognitive component and an affective component. Not surprisingly, the development of trust in leader has been identified as a crucial element in the effectiveness of leaders, individuals, and their organisation. Given its importance in organisations, surprisingly little research has focused on illuminating the positive effects trust in leadership has on employee well-being.

Trust in management mediates the relationship between transformational leadership and employee well-being derives from two separate sources: The first has received substantial empirical support; the second, as mentioned previously, has received no empirical scrutiny and is thus more speculative. First, being able to rely on the skills, abilities, and intentions of those in supervisory positions has been argued to be one of the most important predictors of positive organisational outcomes. Empirical findings support this notion: Trust in leadership is associated, for example, with higher work satisfaction, citisenship behaviours, and performance. These consistently positive findings suggest that by acting as role models who consistently do what is moral and right and not personally beneficial, transformational leaders gain the respect and trust of their followers.

In contrast, we are not aware of any empirical inquiry to date on the relationship between trust in management and psychological well-being. Nonetheless, we suggest that such a link exists for two reasons.

First, positive individual outcomes are consistently associated with trust in management. Second, as organisations face changes of the nature and severity experienced in the past decade, individuals experience uncertainty, anxiety, and fear, all of which have potentially detrimental effects on an individual's well-being.

Thus, we propose that by acting as role models, being committed to employee needs, empowering and encouraging employees to think on their own, and motivating their followers to achieve more than what was thought possible, transformational leaders gain their followers' trust and heighten followers' self-efficacy beliefs. In turn, employees' trust in management and self-efficacy beliefs are associated with their own well-being.

Meaningful Work

A transformational leader can also enable individuals to find positive meaning in their work. We propose that the meaning that individuals make of their work is another one of the mechanisms through which transformational leadership exerts its positive effects on individual well-being. First, we briefly describe the various ways that meaningful work has been conceptualised and measured; then we discuss the research that leads us to suggest that meaningful work mediates this relationship.

The meaning of work is generally conceptualised as the aim or purpose that people have for working. Early research into the meaning that people make of their work found that the economic function of work is but one of many meanings that work may have and is, in fact, not generally the most salient meaning of work MOW International Research Team.

Meaning has been conceptualised and measured in many different ways. While we cannot summarise this body of literature adequately here, we point to a few of the main conceptualisations. Meaning may be conceptualised as existing on multiple levels. Individuals may find a certain specific meaning in their current job. They may also espouse meaning in relation to work in general. These measures entail a broader sense of what work should provide in terms of purpose, as well as some indication of the value of work in relation to other aspects of life. Orientation toward work has been conceptualised as intrinsic versus extrinsic motivation. In the job characteristics model, meaningful work is conceptualised as a critical psychological state resulting from a job that is high in task significance, task identity, and skill variety. We posit that it is this higher purpose that a transformational leader instills in followers, and, as we discuss later, it is this connection that we believe contributes to enhanced well-being.

The theory of transformational leadership suggests several avenues through which the meaning of work can be positively transformed. Transformational leaders raise followers' levels of morality to "more principled levels of judgment" and activate higher order needs in followers. The intellectual stimulation dimension of transformational leadership allows the transformation of crises or stressful situations to challenges. Finally, stress levels of followers may be reduced because of a sense of identity with a social support network that is created through the use of individualised consideration. The verbal cues that individuals in the environment give us about our work are very powerful. The transformational leader is likely to provide positive verbal cues to followers.

Research has established an association between transformational leadership and various measures of meaningful work. Transformational leadership has been found to have a positive impact on congruence of values between leaders and followers, on intrinsic motivation, on belief in a higher purpose of work, and indirectly on job involvement through procedural justice perceptions. Transformational leadership has also been shown to be negatively associated with work alienation.

Evidence of a positive link between the meaning of work and well-being is mixed. Some studies have found that job involvement may exacerbate negative health outcomes in certain cases. Yet, there are also studies that find a positive link between the meaning of work and well-being. Experiencing higher job involvement has been found to be negatively related to burnout, and in a recent longitudinal study, the meaning of work was found to explain 32% of the variance in psychological benefits derived from the experience of deployment in Bosnia. Future research is necessary to confirm these associations and to establish empirically our belief that transformational leadership affects well-being via enhancing the meaning of work.

Organisational and Occupational Identity

A final mediating mechanism through which we believe transformational leadership enhances well-being is organisational and/or occupational identity. Social identity theory states that an individual's self-concept is composed of a personal identity, which encompasses idiosyncratic characteristics, and a social identity, which encompasses the salient groups to which an individual belongs. Social identification is "the perception of belongingness to a group classification". An individual possessing a positive self-concept potentially experiences more positive well-being. Hence, we hypothesise that enhancing organisational or occupational identity in turn positively affects well-being.

In terms of an individual's sense of belonging in the work domain, two of the salient groups to which we belong are the organisation and our occupation. Organisational identification has been defined as "a perceived oneness with an organisation and the experience of the organisation's successes and failures as one's own". We define occupational identity in a similar fashion: a sense of oneness with an occupational group.

To our knowledge, there have been no empirical investigations of the links between transformational leadership and occupational or organisational identity. Yet, theoretically, transformational leaders have the potential to positively influence how individuals perceive the defining characteristics of the organisation as well as the occupational group to which they belong. Through transformational leadership, the needs, values, preferences, and aspirations of followers evolve from self to collective interests. Specifically, Bass suggests that the charismatic dimensions transform participation in organisational efforts from satisfying the self-interests of the follower to an "expression of membership and identity with a social collective." The dimensions of idealised influence and inspirational motivation are most likely to inspire positive identification—whether with the organisation or the occupation.

The positive impact of organisational identification on well-being of individuals and organisations has been recognised in past research. However, because of a lack of attention to occupations in organisational research, there have been fewer investigations of occupational identity. There is indirect evidence that occupational identity impacts positively on well-being. One study of cancer patients found that being able to return to a work role that was important gave people a sense of control. Possession of positive student identity was also found to be positively related to self-esteem in another study. The influence of transformational leadership on this process is conceptually plausible, yet remains empirically untested.

REFERENCES

Hedges, L. V., & Olkin, I. (1984). Nonparametric estimators of effect size in meta-analysis. *Psychological Bulletin, 96*, 573-580.

Hunter, J.E., Schmidt, F. L., & Pearlman, K. (1981). Task differences as moderators of aptitude test validity in selection: A red herring. *Journal of Applied Psychology, 66*, 166-185.

Law, K. S., Schmidt, F. L., & Hunter, J. E. (1994). A test of two refinements in procedures for meta-analysis. *Journal of Applied Psychology, 79*, 978-986.

Rosenthal, R. (1995). Writing meta-analytic reviews. *Psychological Bulletin, 118*, 183-192.

6

Individual Differences

The scientific successes of evolutionary psychology have been most prominent in domains such as survival sexuality mating strategies sexual conflict parenting kinship cooperation and aggression. These theoretical and empirical advances, however, have been achieved primarily at the levels of species-typical and sex-differentiated adaptations. Personality traits and other individual differences—profound and integral to human psychology— have been relatively neglected, with some notable exceptions. Indeed, it is only recently that cogent evolutionary analyses have been devoted to explaining individual differences within nonhuman species.

The key question is this: How can evolutionary psychology successfully explain personality and individual differences? To begin answering this question, one might find it useful to first examine why individual differences have been neglected and why they are so important that they cannot be neglected.

There are important reasons for this neglect, starting with a paucity of powerful theories. Cogent evolutionary theories exist for predicting and explaining sex differences—the most notable being the theory of sexual selection. Evolutionary theories of species-typical adaptations, such as kin-selection theory and the theory of reciprocal altruism, also provide powerful tools. Evolutionary psychologists have synthesised these theories with principles of modern psychology to create unique theories such as social-contract theory, sexual-strategies theory, and error-management theory, which, in turn, have led to important empirical discoveries such as adaptive cognitive biases.

Another reason for the neglect of individual differences can be traced to the foundational assumption in evolutionary biology that natural selection has reduced or eliminated heritable individual differences because traits that are advantageous tend to spread over time to fixation and become species-typical. This assumption seemed reasonable 20 years ago, but it has been seriously challenged by key theoretical developments in evolutionary biology and advances in evolutionary foundations of psychology.

Importannce of Individual Differences

Individual differences acquire importance for several reasons— some empirical and some theoretical. First, profound and consequential individual differences have been well documented—individual differences in personality characteristics general intelligence and more specific abilities mating strategies political attitudes religiosity body type mate value, and many others. Second, researchers have shown that most of these individual differences have a heritable component and show stability over time. Virtually all personality characteristics, for example, show heritabilities in the range of 50% and substantial cross-time stability, even over spans of decades. Third, these stable individual differences have been shown to have important consequences for evolutionarily relevant outcomes, such as survival, mating success, offspring production, and parenting.

Fourth, individuals often differ substantially within their own sex on characteristics that exhibit well-documented sex differences. In the domain of mating, individuals differ profoundly in the mating strategies they pursue. Some pursue a long-term mating strategy marked by lifelong monogamy. Others pursue a short-term mating strategy marked by frequent partner switching. And still others pursue a mixed mating strategy, with one long-term mate combined with some short-term sex on the side. Although many individuals prefer to be higher rather than lower in status hierarchies, people differ profoundly in the strategies they use to attain status, in the actual relative rank they attain, and even in the preferred rank to which they aspire. "Cheater-detection" adaptations, to take another example, prevent one from being exploited in social exchanges. And some individuals are more exploitable than others, enabling adaptations for exploitation to flourish. All of these empirical observations tell us that individual differences cannot and should not be ignored.

Theoretically, individual differences are also profoundly important. Individual differences are pivotal to the vast majority of social adaptive problems. Consider selecting a mate. Constants simply do not count. Species-typical characteristics become invisible when solving the adaptive problem of mate selection. Only differences between individuals count—in attractiveness, intelligence, dependability, health, agreeableness, ambition, empathy, and so forth. As a consequence, humans have evolved specialised adaptations for tracking and acting on these individual differences: difference-detecting adaptations. These adaptations reveal the specific differences that are crucial to monitor because they have been vital to human survival and reproduction over a long period of evolutionary time.

Life-History Theory

Each individual has finite time and energy budgets. Effort allocated to solving one adaptive problem precludes effort allocated to other adaptive problems. Life-history theory is a broad formulation of the major trade-offs in an individual's life with respect to capturing and allocating energy. Energy can be allocated toward reproduction, which subsumes all of the effort required to successfully select, attract, and retain a mate, at least long enough for successful conception.

Because energy is finite, there are trade-offs in the adaptive problems to which it is allocated. Energy an individual allocates to bodily maintenance, for example, cannot be used to invest in children. This broad scheme, of course, represents an oversimplification because some forms of energy expenditure can contribute to two or more adaptive problems. The effort a hunter–gatherer male puts into hunting, for example, can provide meat for his own bodily maintenance and growth; increase his social status, rendering him more sexually attractive to potential mates; and provide sustenance for his children and extended kin.

The optimal trade-off between different allocations will undoubtedly differ depending on variables such as one's own qualities, life expectancy, and the total energy an individual has to expend. Those with exceptional fathering talents, for example, might scale back on mating effort. Individuals with bleak mating prospects might ratchet up investment in kin. What is often disparaged as a maladjusted personality marked by impulsivity and lack of self-control instead can be conceptualised within life-history theory as an adaptive stable strategy deployed in response to a realistic appraisal of a shorter time horizon.

Some individual differences represent the different trade-offs that different individuals make with respect to the broad classes of energy allocation as they go through life. Men who happen to be highly sexually attractive to women, for example, sometimes allocate a lion's share of their effort to securing a succession of mates and forgo allocating effort to parenting—a phenomenon also seen in some avian species.

Testosterone is one hormone that facilitates success in intrasexual competition, status striving, and mating effort. It is interesting to note that there is evidence that men's testosterone levels drop following entry into a committed mateship and drop further after they have children. So individual differences in testosterone may be predictably linked to stable individual differences in the effort allocated to mating versus that allocated to parenting, as well as to predictable life-history shifts in the adaptive problems to which individuals allocate effort.

Costly Signaling Theory

Individuals compete with one another in sending signals to others about their quality as a mate, friend, and coalition member. Those perceived as having the highest quality have an advantage in being chosen by the highest quality mates, friends, and coalitions. These social competitions provide incentives for deception.

Any form of deception, however, creates selection for adaptations in signal receivers to detect deception and to discount dishonest signals. Costly signaling theory provides an evolutionary framework for understanding some forms of individual differences. Costly signals tend to be honest signals. Only those in the best condition, be it physical, economic, or energetic, can "afford" to send the signal. In many traditional cultures, for example, men engage in physical contests of various sorts, ranging from wrestling to chest-pounding to ax fighting. Winning these contests, and even the willingness to engage in them, sends a signal to others in the group about the man's physical and psychological quality—his health, strength, athletic prowess, and courage.

Some major individual differences can, in principle, be explained by costly signaling theory. Those lacking resources generally cannot afford to throw lavish parties, pick up the restaurant tab for the group, or give expensive gifts to friends and potential mates. Individual differences in generosity, courage, fidelity, magnanimity, and even possibly traits such as agreeableness and conscientiousness, may be partially explained by a costly signaling theory analysis.

Costly signaling theory can be linked to life-history theory. A male who cannot afford to produce high-quality signals as a short-term mate, for example, might shift to a life-history strategy of heavy investment in one long-term committed mateship. Even the decision of how much energy to expend on costly signals is a life-history decision, suggesting that costly signaling theory and life-history theory can be linked in explaining individual differences.

Balancing Selection

Balancing selection occurs when genetic variation is maintained by selection, such that different levels on a trait dimension are favored, or are adaptive, in different environmental conditions to the same degree. Although all heritable variation ultimately originates from mutations, the different fitness optima of heritable variants over time and space can maintain the heritable variation. Although there are several forms of balancing selection, the two most relevant forms for personality are environmental heterogeneity in fitness optima and frequency-dependent selection.

Environmental Heterogeneity in Fitness Optima If selection pressures vary over time or space, as some of them do, then selection can favor different levels of a personality trait in these different environments. A plausible empirical example comes from a study that assessed the personality traits of people living in mainland Italy and on a number of small islands off the coast of Italy. People inhabiting the small islands for 20 generations or more scored lower on both extraversion and openness to experience than did the recent immigrants and mainlanders with similar historical and cultural backgrounds.

More direct evidence comes from molecular genetic studies, which find that the 7R allele of the DRD4 gene, associated with novelty seeking and extraversion, occurs at dramatically different rates in different geographical regions. It occurs at higher rates in America than in Asia and has been hypothesised to be favored by selection when people migrate to new environments or inhabit resource-rich environments. Migratory populations showed a far higher proportion of long-allele DRD4 genes than did sedentary populations, which could be caused by selective migration of individuals carrying those genes, selective favoring of those genes in the new environments, or both.

Frequency-Dependent Selection

A second type of balancing selection is frequency-dependent selection, which occurs when two or more strategies are maintained within a population at a particular frequency relative to each other, such that the fitness of each strategy decreases as it becomes increasingly common. Biological sex is the most obvious example of frequency-dependent selection. As the ratio of males-to-females in a population increases, the average fitness of males decreases, and vice versa. Frequency-dependent selection has been hypothesised to explain the personality constellation that characterises psychopathy—a cheating strategy that involves exploiting the majority strategy of cooperation and is favored especially in males since it is spread through the success at short-term seduction and abandonment of women.

More generally, competition is typically keenest in resource-rich areas. Selection sometimes favors strategies for accruing resources, be they food, territory, or mates, in domains where competition is less keen and less costly.

The hard work for balancing selection explanations of personality, identifying the specific costs and benefits of different levels of trait dimensions in different environments, remains for the future. Nettle has broken ground on this important task by offering an analysis of the costs and benefits of the personality dimensions captured by the five-factor personality model. Extraversion, for example, appears to confer benefits on some components of fitness, such as success in short-term mating and mate poaching. But extraversion may also carry fitness costs in the currency of survival. Neuroticism, to take another example, could benefit a person by leading to greater vigilance of dangers at a cost to long-term health due to prolonged psychological stress.

Conceptualising environments in terms of the salience and distribution of different adaptive problems offers an extremely promising direction. Indeed, defining situations in terms of adaptive problems may provide a cogent solution to a problem that has long plagued personality psychologists—that of identifying a nonarbitrary way in which to conceptualise situations in the search for personality coherence. Different environments undoubtedly afford different fitness optima on these cost–benefit trade-offs. The threat of social exclusion, for example, may be higher in some social environments than in others. Progress on the big question of understanding individual differences, in short, will require a crisp conceptualisation of situations as defined by adaptive problems and the identification of environments in which different cost–benefit trade-offs are favored.

Mutation Load

Each human carries mutations, which can occur on any of the approximately 25,000 genes that characterise the human genome. Some mutations are selectively neutral and can be maintained because they do not disrupt the functioning of the brain or other organs. A few provide adaptive advantage and are favored by selection. Other mutations are disruptive. Conservative estimates suggest that, on average, humans carry at least 500 brain-disruptive mutations. Although selection eventually weeds out harmful mutations, those that are only mildly harmful may not be purged by selection for many generations. Evidence suggests that the heritability of some traits originates from individual differences in mutation load, which can plausibly explain some harmful mental disorders such as schisophrenia and autism.

It is also possible that individual differences in mutation load can explain some personality variation within the normal range. Although a mutation load explanation of individual differences may seem less interesting in that mutations merely add random noise to functional systems, the maladaptive noise they create at the phenotypic level may provide individual differences input into adaptations designed to make critical social selections such as choosing a mate, friend, coalition partner, or even a kin member for investment. Consequently, adaptations that track individual differences in mate value—one type of difference-detecting mechanism—may actually be tracking individual differences in mutation load. Mutation load thus can create relationship load. In these ways, the mutation load explanation becomes more interesting theoretically in the broader context of explaining individual differences within an evolutionary psychological framework.

Contingent Shifts

Another key mode of explaining individual differences comes from hypotheses that invoke environmentally contingent or culturally contingent shifts. This mode of explaining individual differences is distinct from the process described above as environmental heterogeneity in fitness optima. Environmental heterogeneity in fitness optima refers to the process by which natural selection produces heritable individual differences— different alleles are differentially selected within different environments. In contrast, the concept of contingent shifts refers to selection for species-typical psychological mechanisms that are flexibly responsive to changes in environmental conditions.

Some of these may be subsumed under life-history theory, as when a man shifts to a more cautious, risk-averse strategy after becoming a father. Others may be subsumed by costly signaling theory, as when an environmentally contingent increase in mate value affords a greater ability to emit costly signals. Still others come from situation-specific shifts, such as becoming more risk-taking during times of famine when food resources are scarce and require dangerous action to obtain.

Contingent shifts also can occur in response to one's heritable phenotypic characteristics, which has been characterised as "reactive heritability". Males with larger body size at age 3, both in height and bulk, tend to be less agreeable and more aggressive at age 11. The key point is that contingent shifts can occur in response to individual phenotypic qualities as well as to external environmental conditions.

Life-history theory, costly signaling theory, environmental heterogeneity, frequency-dependent selection, mutation load, and environment-contingent and phenotypic-contingent shifts in strategy all provide theoretical options for explaining personality and individual differences.

Strategic Individual differences

One key toward a deeper understanding of personality and individual differences will come from changing the ways in which psychologists conceptualise them. Specifically, at least some personality differences can be conceptualised as alternative strategies for solving recurrent adaptive problems. Some individual differences may reflect differences in the strategies individuals use to solve these adaptive problems.

Consider an adaptive problem all humans confront—that of negotiating status hierarchies. Hawley discovered individual differences in strategies used to achieve position in dominance hierarchies, focusing on the key distinction between prosocial and coercive strategies. Extraverts tended to emit positive externalities to get ahead. Those low on agreeableness tended to use deception and manipulation to get ahead. And those high on conscientiousness tended to use sheer hard work to advance in hierarchies.

Another adaptive problem involves extracting resources from other people who inhabit one's social environment. Buss discovered that individual differences in personality captured by the five factor model are reliably linked to 12 different influence strategies people use for securing resources from others. Those low on agreeableness, for example, are especially likely to use coercive strategies to get what they want. People low on emotional stability are especially likely to use regression strategies to get what they want. And those scoring low on extraversion are especially likely to use monetary rewards and self-abasement to extract resources from others. Some personality traits, in short, reflect individual differences in strategies used to solve social adaptive problems such as attaining dominance and extracting resources.

A related development along these lines is conceptualising personality dispositions as "motivational individual reaction norms" to specific classes of environmental circumstances or adaptive problems. Denissen and Penke propose an explanatory theory of the five factor personality model that makes it less of a purely descriptive model. Denissen and Penke also propose that conscientiousness reflects a strategy of tenacity versus frame shifting under distracting circumstances.

Another conceptual tact involves breaking away from or adding to traditional conceptions of personality, such as those anchored in the five-factor model. Individual differences in sociosexuality provide one example of an evolutionarily framed stable individual difference. Another example from the sexual domain involves other stable sexual strategies that are beyond the five-factor model or only weakly correlated with it.

An evolutionary psychological formulation of environments as the distribution and salience of adaptive problems each individual confronts will provide a much-needed advance on a conceptual problem that has plagued the field of personality since its inception—how to provide a nonarbitrary formulation of situations in the search for personality coherence. Because personality differences appear to be most profound within social species, identifying social adaptive problems will form the core of this formulation. Social adaptive problems include threats from within the group as well as threats from outside the group. They will range from the adaptive problem of mate selection to the adaptive problems faced in the aftermath of a break-up. And they will vary developmentally along with life-history shifts in energy allocation from growth to mating to parenting to extended kin investment.

In summary, scientifically satisfactory answers to the big question of explaining personality and individual differences may entail conceptualising some personality differences as strategic differences; conceptualising different environments in terms of the distribution and salience of adaptive problems, many of which will be social in nature; and identifying the costs, benefits, and trade-offs of strategic individual differences in these different problem-defined environments. Although we're a long distance from answering the question of how to explain personality and individual differences, modern evolutionary psychology provides some powerful conceptual tools for doing so.

References

Campbell, J.P. (1990). Modeling the performance prediction problem in industrial and organizational psychology. In M.D. Dunnette & L.M. Hough (Eds.), *Handbook of industrial and organizational psychology* (2nd ed., Vol 1, pp. 687-732). Palo Alto, CA: Consulting Psychologists Press.

Hunter, J. E. (1986). Cognitive ability, cognitive aptitude, job knowledge, and job performance. *Journal of Vocational Behavior, 29*, 340-362.

Jex, S. M., & Britt, T. W. (2008). *Organizational Psychology*. Hoboke, New Jersey: John Wiley & Sons, Inc.

O'Driscoll, M. P., & Cooper, C. L. (1994). Coping with work-related stress: A critique of existing measures and proposal for an alternative methodology. *Journal of Occupational and Organizational Psychology, 67*, 343-354.

7

Work Motivation

Is it possible that half of those who admit that they could work much harder might actually decide to increase their performance by 20 percent if they were adequately motivated? The best evidence suggests that highly significant performance increases are possible when motivational strategies are implemented. Stolovitch, Clark and Condly found that financial incentive programs increase work performance more than 20 percent and the more effective programs produce increases in the 40 percent range.

Work motivation is the process that initiates and maintains goal-directed performance. It energises our thinking, fuels our enthusiasm and colors our positive and negative emotional reactions to work and life. Motivation generates the mental effort that drives us to apply our knowledge and skills. Without motivation, even the most capable person will refuse to work hard. Motivation prevents or nudges us to convert intention into action and start doing something new or to restart something we've done before. It also controls our decisions to persist at a specific work goal in the face of distractions and the press of other priorities. Finally, motivation leads us to invest more or less cognitive effort to enhance both the quality and quantity of our work performance.

It is crucial to note that motivation does not directly influence work performance. Instead, motivation leads us to use our knowledge and skills and apply them effectively to work tasks. Successful performance always involves the cooperation of motivation and knowledge in supportive work environments. Without adequate knowledge, motivation alone does not increase useful performance. Thus adequate motivation is necessary, but not sufficient for effective performance.

Cause of Effective Motivation

After more than a century of research and argument, motivation researchers and practitioners now begin to agree that motivation is the result of our beliefs about what makes us successful and effective. We all value the goals, working conditions and incentives that we believe will contribute to our success. We avoid situations that will prevent us from achieving our goals. Whether we call motivational tools "reinforcement", "incentives", "drivers", "inducements" or by some other quasi-technical name, they only motivate when they are perceived as making us successful or effective. Conversely, we avoid conditions that we think will delay, inhibit or prevent the attainment of objectives.

The variety problem. What makes motivation a complex issue is that different individuals and groups have very different beliefs about the nature of "success" and about what supports or prevents success. People working in teams may define success differently than when they are working alone.

One way to think the variety of personality types measured by the Myers Briggs scale, the American Psychological Association's "Big Five" and many of the other style measures is that they measure our values. Some people value reflective, analytical and organised approaches while others value impulsive, expressive, intuitive reactions. Many people work for money and/or recognition and others will work for the sheer joy of doing something well or learning something new. Some of us are very effective at regulating our own motivation by ignoring the demotivators and creating the conditions that create personal success. Most of us work with different values and styles in different situations. How can we make sense of such breathtaking variety and turn it to our benefit as performance technologists?

The variety solution - universal motivators. In any given situation where we want to increase work motivation, we must determine what will convince people to start doing something new or different, increase their persistence at an important task and invest mental effort. They must believe that the motivator driving their enhanced performance will directly or indirectly contribute significantly to what they need to feel successful and effective. The motivator that works has to cost less than the value of the increased performance and it must meet both ethical and legal requirements. While organisations may need to tailor these universal motivators and demotivators for individuals and teams, there are finite number of powerful doable, cost-effective, ethical and legal strategies for increasing work motivation for nearly everyone.

Managerial Practices that Destroy Motivation

There are at least five elements of work environments that most researchers agree are the main destroyers of motivation. While a discussion of what kills motivation is a negative exercise, it is critical to emphasise that some very common and popular features of organisations hurt the work motivation of many people who work in them.

1) *Avoid even the appearance of dishonesty, hypocrisy, and unfairness*: Organisations don't have to lie or cheat or be unfair - they only have to be perceived in this way to destroy motivation. Perception is nearly everything in motivation. Managers often feel that they must tell "innocent untruths", refuse to keep promises as work conditions change, or favor their friends. Most of us do not believe that when we do these things we are "lying" or being "hypocritical" or "unfair."

   Private perceptions control personal motivation, not publically shared views or generally accepted "reality". When people perceive their treatment as unfair, dishonest or hypocritical, the best we can hope for is that they will act mature, ignore those conditions and work hard despite it all. Yet, even the most mature people are not going to work as hard when they experience dishonest and unfair behaviour directed at them personally. Motivation is enhanced when everyone in an organisation avoids even the appearance of unfairness, prejudice, dishonesty or hypocracy.

2) *Discourage vague, impossible and constantly changing performance goals*: In the absence of a clear vision leading to well-defined business and performance goals, people substitute their own goals and their goals may not support the organisation. Vagueness and inconsistency in a work environment lead most people to assume that "anything goes." Without clear performance goals and feedback, people are not committed to work and are not inclined to give their best effort. Increased work motivation is supported by concrete and challenging work goals that are focused on the near term. Everyone should know what they are expected to do this month and next. Conversely, impossible "stretch goals" often damage motivation. The only exception to this rule is when people assume that the organisation "could not be serious" and so interpret an impossible goal as instructions to "work harder". Goals must be challenging and difficult but work goals should not be described in a way that leads people to perceived them as impossible to achieve. The most motivating goals have "3C" qualities: Challenging Concrete and Current.

3) *Eliminate unnecessary rules, policy and work barriers*:
Many studies point to the huge variety of arbitrary and seemingly unnecessary rules and cumbersome policies as one of the major demotivators at work. It is important to ask about evidence for the benefit of all work rules and what might be lost if they were eliminated. What is gained by rules that people can't talk or eat in certain areas? Why can't people decorate their work space in ways that suit them? Do we have solid evidence beyond our preferences that dress codes are necessary and that they add value to a business?

4) *Discourage constant competition with everyone.*
Focused competition can be a very motivating experience for some people. Sales people seem to thrive on it and most people who are raised in Western cultural traditions like a bit of it. Yet constant, intense rivalry can support a destructive level of internal competition and focuses attention and energy away from business goals. The performance improvement methods they surveyed attempted to get members of work teams to bond, collaborate, and

work efficiently toward common goals by competing with other teams. When the Academy released its findings, it was not surprising to learn that many of the most popular team-building programs had succeeded in increasing collaboration and cooperation between team members but the teams were competing in a nearly suicidal fashion with other teams in the same organisation. Consider the possibility that motivational techniques other than competition might achieve similar or greater results with less risk.

5) *Replace negative and/or prejudicial feedback with gap-focused feedback*:

Some managers seem to believe that in order to "keep people on their toes" they have to watch carefully until people make a mistake and then jump on them - or remind them of their past mistakes whenever they are acting independently or seem overly satisfied with something they've done.

Negative emotion is one of the biggest killers of motivation. A recent international review of performance feedback research studies found that negative feedback that focused on mistakes actually depressed performance. This happened in one-third of all feedback research studies conducted both in natural settings and in the laboratory. Effective performance feedback was focused on describing and closing the gap between goals and current performance. When feedback emphasises negative qualities of the performer, performance deteriorates. The finding that poor feedback was obvious in two-thirds of all well-planned research studies suggests that it may even be more prevalent in practice since researchers tend to select typical strategies to test in experiments.

Motivational Strategies that Work for Everyone

Most of the strategies that contribute most to developing motivation are relatively easy to implement and cost very little. The three motivational "push points" that work for everyone are to build realistic levels of self-confidence, positive emotion and effective personal values for work tasks.

1. *Help people develop self-confidence in their work skills*. A primary motivational goal is to support a high level of personal

confidence in everyone's belief about their own ability to achieve their performance goals. People's belief about whether "I have the skills required to succeed at this task" is perhaps the most important factor in our commitment to work tasks and the quality and quantity of mental effort people invest in their work.

When people lack confidence that they can succeed at a specific goal, they will not choose to tackle that goal. If they have started to work on the goal, they may find a way to convince themselves to switch to less vital tasks, invest very little mental effort or argue about their assignment. If people are overconfident, they will not invest much mental effort in tasks and also not take responsibility when they fail or make mistakes. Everyone needs very high levels of confidence about their job skills. However, if overconfidence turns to arrogance, they are tempted to ignore their mistakes and treat all very novel challenges as if they are routine and familiar.

To help people build self-confidence we must constantly check with them to learn their concerns and what will help them build confidence. The real danger here is that people believe that others are "like us" and so will respond positively to the confidence builders that we prefer. The best assumption is that people are not like us and that "other people" are most likely to be motivated by very different values than our own and that "other people's" values are not "wrong or stupid," only different.

2. *Create a positive emotional environment at work.* Emotions are usually ignored in discussions about motivation but they are very important. Positive emotions, such as happiness, humor and joy, support and enhance work commitment and negative emotions, such as anger, extreme frustration and depression, kill it. Yet it is not necessary for everyone to be happy in order to be committed. It is more important that people are not excessively unhappy, angry or depressed about work issues.

   Yet different people sometimes have very different ideas about what helps them have positive emotions or get rid of negative feelings. Even if people were more alike each other, we cannot always do a great deal to modify extremely negative work emotions. The effort invested in creating a positive, enjoyable work climate can pay off in increased work commitment for many people because the result is less negativity about work.

Gordon Bower has surveyed the research on the impact of a positive mood on performance. Bower emphasised asking people what would make their work environment more "enjoyable". His research could be summarised as recommending the following ways to support positive emotions toward work for everyone:

- Engage people in decisions about the esthetic design of their collective workplace. Invest in a bright, lively, positive environmental design. Let people decorate their personal work space if the decoration will not interfere with other people or violate important policy.
- Allow people to listen privately to music while they work if listening does not decrease work efficiency or interfere with others work.
- Eliminate rules and policies that reduce work enjoyment without providing a measured benefit that is greater than the loss of commitment they cause.
- Encourage everyone, including supervisors and managers, to be enthusiastic, positive, and supportive. Cynical, negative, pessimistic and "sour grape" styles may be fashionable in some organisational cultures, but they do not encourage positive emotion or work commitment.

3. *Support the development of strong personal values for performance goals*

All of the advice on performance motivation up to this point can be viewed as ways to enhance people's beliefs that if they make a strong commitment and persist at their performance goals, they will become more effective. Personal confidence and emotions are intimately connected with effectiveness beliefs. Our confidence is a measure of our belief about how our own ability or how organisational processes will support our success and effectiveness.

Values are one of the three powerful ways people express their views about what they expect will make them effective. People value what they believe helps them, and they reject what they believe stands in their way. Values can be viewed as preferences that lead people to more quickly adopt a course of action and persist in the face of distractions. Of course, different people have different values. The goal here is to increase people's work commitment by suggesting connections between their own values and the benefit of achieving work goals.

CREATING VALUE FOR WORK

Eccles and Wigfield present evidence that most people use three different types of values:

— *Interest value*. People will more easily and quickly choose to do what interests them the most. Many people are generally interested in mastering a new skill or adding to their expertise. This more "intrinsic" interest pattern often characterises the most effective workers. Others are more interested in impressing managers with their capability. This more "performance" oriented style can also be useful under some conditions.

— *Skill value*. Most people seem more willing to do those things that they believe challenge one of their special "skills." So people who see themselves as more analytical like brain teasers and difficult analytical problems and tasks.

— So much of what we do is chosen not because we love it or can excel at it but because we want the benefits that come when we finish and to avoid the negative consequences of avoiding or delaying. This is called "*utility value*" and it shifts a person's focus from "means" to "ends." It asks people to focus on the benefits of finishing the task and not on their lack of interest or discomfort about the means to reach the end. Utility value can be enhanced by describing the realistic benefits of completing a less desired task or goal and the risks of avoiding it. Do not inflate either the benefits or the risks.

Financial incentives that create value. Another highly effective way to increase motivation for work is to provide financial incentives for exceeding past performance. The overall results of the large body of studies that are published in reputable journals suggest that cash and other tangible incentives can be very powerful and relatively inexpensive ways to increase the value people place on work goals.

To most researchers who study this question, the evidence is clear that financial or other tangible incentives can significantly increase people's work performance by increasing their motivation. For the incentives to provide maximum benefit, the performance level must be very challenging not routine or easy, but also not perceived as impossible. In much of the research, an "impossible" task is defined as one where the probability of success is less than fifteen percent.

Four types of incentive programs. The four types of incentive programs are:

1) *Quota schemes*. When organisations use a "quota scheme," they appear to get the largest motivational benefit. Quotas offer additional bonus pay for work that exceeds a previous level achieved by the individual, team or organisation, or by another organisation.
2) *Piece rate schemes*. The second most effective use of tangible incentives is in "piece rate" schemes where a set amount of output, for example, the manual assembly of one electronics board, is tied to a set rate of pay. Quota and piece rate schemes are often combined to get the benefit of both approaches.
3) *Tournament schemes*. The third ranking incentive approach is "tournament schemes" where pay is linked to performance rankings based on competition between people doing the same job. This plan is often used to motivate sales staff. The factors that are thought to diminish the effects of tournament incentives are the fact that only capable people tend to "play". Another problem here is that competition sometimes leads to attempts to sabotage the efforts of competitors, thus reducing the overall benefit to the organisation.
4) *Flat rate schemes* pr fixed pay schemes are the least effective overall. It is ironic that "work for a set salary" is the best example of a flat rate incentive system. Here we pay people for "full time" work, usually pegged at forty hours a week.

Disputes about incentive systems: Many of the disputes about pay incentives focus on evidence, drawn largely from studies with children in classrooms, that our personal interest in work tasks decrease when tangible incentives are used to reward work. In the future, the argument goes, people who are paid more for interesting work, will work for extra pay and not because they are interested. The best advice is not to provide tangible incentives to people who are already achieving business goals without tangible rewards, unless there is an excellent financial reason to exceed business goals at the possible risk of future "interest" motivation.

Team Motivation

To this point, the discussion has emphasised motivational strategies that work for nearly everyone or that can be translated to work with different people. Yet most people work in teams some of the time and it appears that when we are in teams, we must consider additional motivational issues. Al Bandura has devoted a considerable part of his career studying ways to motivate people who work in groups.

Two key features of team motivation expertise and collaboration. When people work in teams they encounter two issues that can either help or hinder their team spirit and motivation; first is their belief about whether other team members have the variety of skills and knowledge necessary to achieve team goals; and, second is their expectation about whether the team will collaborate effectively to get the job done. Each member of the team has to be viewed as able to make her/his own contribution to team goals. When people doubt that one or more of their team members are competent and when they believe that the capabilities of the other members are necessary to get the job done, motivation suffers dramatically. Directly confronting the confidence issue is recommended if the questioned member has expertise that is not appreciated. If expertise is lacking or questionable, team members may have to be replaced. The best way to prevent this problem is to address it carefully when teams are selected.

Even when teams trust each others' expertise, team members may doubt that the team can work together effectively. Since collaboration is an essential requirement for team success, uncooperative, highly independent but talented players can wreck team motivation by refusing to work effectively with other members.

Social loafing in teams. Team members who refuse to carry their weight also challenge team motivation. This phenomenon is called "social loafing". Some team members seem to think that when they work collectively, they do not need to work as hard. Social loafing has been the subject of performance research since the turn of the century. Early studies examined how much force individuals used to pull on a rope when asked to "pull as hard as possible". In every case, when additional people were added to the rope, each individual seemed to pull a bit less forcefully.

Correcting social loafing through individual assessment. The "loafing" effect can be eliminated very quickly and effectively with one strategy. When we assess the individual contribution of each member of a team, whether they are pulling a rope or designing a new product, social loafing disappears. Thus, another crucial support for team motivation is to inform team members that the organisation will assess the individual contributions of each member of every team rather than only assessing the achievement of the entire team.

Motivational Needs and Expectations

Main needs and expectations to be taken into account in considering the motivation of people at work are described below.

Most of the working people have their physiological, security and belongingness needs satisfied. Their behaviour is mostly directed towards satisfying the fourth order needs of power, prestige and status. These needs have been found to influence work behaviour of people in different work settings. These needs are described below:

The need for activity is a desire to be constantly doing things. This kind of person is a hard worker.

The need for extension is a desire to be helpful to others and to provide one's services to the organisation or nation.

The need for dependence is the need to consult others before making any decision. Such people feel insecure and want to be protected.

The need for independence is a desire to do things individually and to be one's own self. They prefer freedom. Like to make decisions. They dislike interference.

The need for power is desire to influence others and gain control over them. Such people like to lead and enjoy giving directions to others. They are argumentative and seek leadership positions.

They need for aggression creates a desire to dominate others and to demonstrate one's own strength at times, even physically. These people talk loud, are argumentative and may get into physical fights.

The need for status and prestige is a desire to be respected and treated with deference specially by others in the social situations. These people are status conscious, they may run for offices and show authoritarian tendencies when working with others.

The need for recognition demands recognition for one's accomplishments. These people may be completely demotivated if their work is not immediately recognised.

The need for achievement is a concern for excellence. People dominated by this need are generally active, work hard, set high goals, take challenging tasks, desire pleasure from doing difficult things and look for quality.

In addition to the nine important needs mentioned above, there are two others that fall into second and third order needs that are important in the work place. These are the need for security and need for affiliation.

The need for security is the need to be secure about one's own livelihood and to be sure to continue to have it, the domination by this need calls for economic security and causes frustration at lack of job.

The need for affiliation is a concern for establishing or maintaining warm and affectionate relations with others. To fulfill this need people join groups, invite people and develop attachment.

The satisfaction of these eleven needs mentioned above are important in the work place. The organisation must provide opportunities to satisfy these needs to ensure a motivating environment in the work place. Understanding these needs and behaviour indicators of these motives help us to understand the people. This must be appreciated and the working environment must be so structured that it provides opportunities for satisfying these needs. If these are considered carefully then there can be high motivation of people at work.

It is important to create conditions where scientists and other workers' energies are not expanded totally in meeting their basic needs, but where opportunities exist to satisfy higher order needs. Create a climate for interdependent work rather than dependency. In the work place create a competitive climate through recognition of good work and a productive climate through personal example.

Various studies have been conducted for the management of motivation in the work situation. It is worthwhile to examine the results of some of these studies. The first of these studies is the Hawthorne experiment. In 1924, efficiency experts at the Hawthorne, Illinois, plant of the Western Electric Company designed a research programe to study the effects of illumination on productivity.

Hawthorne Studies

In the initial study of Hawthorne, efficiency experts assumed that increases in illumination would result in higher output. Two groups of employees were selected: an experimental or test group, which worked under varying degrees of light, and a control group, which worked under normal illumination conditions in the plant. As lighting power was increased, the output of the test group went up an anticipated. Unexpectedly, however, the output of the control group went up also without any increase in light. Mayo and his associates discovered that the answer to this phenomenon was not in the production conditions aspect of the experiment, but in the human aspect. They no longer viewed themselves as isolated individuals but had become members of a congenial, cohesive work group. The relationships, that developed elicited feelings of affiliation, competence and achievement. This led to the conclusion that the most significant factor affecting organisational productivity is the interpersonal relationships that develop on the job, not just pay and working conditions.

Theory X and Theory Y

According to the Mc Gregor, traditional organisation with its centralised decision making, superior – subordinate pyramid, and external control of work, is based upon certain assumptions about human nature and human motivation. These assumptions which he describes as Theory X, are, that most people prefer to be directed, are not interested in assuming responsibility, and want safety above all. Accompanying this philosophy is the belief that people are motivated by money, fringe benefits, and the threat of punishment. He felt that management needed practices based on a more accurate understanding of human nature and motivation. As a result of these feelings he developed an alternate theory of human behaviour called Theory Y. This theory assumes that people are not, by nature lasy and unreliable. It postulates that people can be basically self-directed and creative at work if properly motivated. Therefore, it should be the essential task of management to unleash this potential in individuals. The properly motivated people can achieve their own goals best by directing their own efforts towards accomplishing organisational goals.

The impression that one might get from the discussion of Theory – X and Theory – Y is that managers who accept Theory X usually direct, control, and closely supervise people, while Theory Y managers are supportive and facilitating. This kind of conclusion could lead to the trap of thinking that Theory X is 'bad' and Theory Y is 'good'. Although the best assumptions for a manager to have may be Theory Y, it may not be appropriate to behave consistent with those assumptions all the time. Managers may have Theory Y assumptions about human nature, but they may find it necessary to behave in a very directive, controlling manner with some people in the short run to help them "grow up" in a developmental sense, until they are truly Theory Y people.

Motivation – Hygiene Theory

Hersberg found that people have two different categories of needs in the work situation, and these are essentially independent of each other and affect behaviour in different ways. He found that when people felt dissatisfied with their jobs, they were concerned about the environment in which they were working. On the other hand, when people felt good about their jobs, this had to do with the work itself. Hersberg called the first category of needs hygiene or maintenance factors: Hygiene because they describe people's environment and serve their primary function of preventing job dissatisfaction: maintenance because they are never completely satisfied – they have to continue to be maintained.

The hygiene factors if absent will cause dissatisfaction but their presence does not create positive motivation. In the presence of satisfactory hygiene factors, motivators are necessary to stimulate positive motivation. Satisfaction of the motivators, however, will permit an individual to grow and develop in a mature way, often implementing an increase in ability. Thus, hygiene factors affect an individual's willingness or motivation and motivators impact an individual's ability.

Needs Theory

Another model for work related motivation is that of MC Clelland. He studied the basic needs and concerns, people frequently express, and divided them into three groups: People with a high need for affiliation. Every one has each of these needs to some degree, but seldom in the same strength. A person may be high in the need for power, low in the need for achievement, and moderate in the need for power. Such people would tend to think more about friendship than about doing a good job or controlling others.

Competitive behaviour results from high need for power and collaborative behaviour results from a high need for affiliation while competitive and / or collaborative behaviour may result from high need for achievement. We often define a situation as being a 'Sero-sum' power game. Our definition causes us to behave in a certain way – i.e. to compete instead of collaborative in order to achieve our goals. But this does not mean that competitive behaviour is always bad and collaborative behaviour is always good. The salient issues are:

1. Under what conditions are the two forms of behaviour appropriate?
2. What kinds of factors cause us to misread a given situation and what are the consequences.

Unfortunately, most of the social situations we find ourselves in are neither purely competitive nor purely collaborative. One complication is that we frequently have to play the competitive and collaborative games simultaneously, such as when we are trying to problem-solve with the same persons with whom we are competing for promotion. However, it is fortunate that in the ICAR personnel policy, at least at the lower level it is laid out that promotion is person oriented and not post oriented. Unfortunately, at the higher level, there is no career advancement by assessment and promotions irrespective of the number of posts. Thus the promotion is post oriented where all people compete to fill a limited number of higher research management positions.

A second complication arises from the fact that we frequently cannot accurately diagnose a situation as competitive or collaborative until we know how the other participants are viewing it and how they will behave.

Some people may approach every situation as if it were a competitive game, e.g. they will transport every discussion into a debate. Others will approach every situation as if were a collaborative game. The first type can be called cynical, the second naïve, and the third realistic.

In which category do you and your colleagues fall?

The common problem we generally face today is cynicism – we characteristically approach situations as if they are competitive even when they are not. The conflicts between the senior and junior scientists and the problems of sharing the facilities result from this attitude. It is now time to wonder if the game might have some collaborative aspects.

Intrinsic Motivation

The most prominent suggestion for organising firms is to introduce market elements and prices through such methods as profit centers, spin-offs, or holdings. Intrinsic motivation is not simply additive to the motivation induced by prices (extrinsic incentives). Rather, under some conditions the use of the price system undermines intrinsic motivation (crowding-out effect), making motivation endogenous to organisational forms.

Increasingly, firms are being restructured by introducing market elements such as profit centers, divisional units, or holdings. The idea is to exploit the advantages of the price mechanism by making the exchanges between the actors or departments more explicit and by rewarding employees according to their contribution to the firm's profit. This strategy corresponds to a view of firms as the governance structure "of last resort, to be employed when all else fails"

What "non-market" organisation means is left unexplored. The resource-based theory of the firm, which is the leading alternative approach to the economic view, is also vague with respect to organisational forms. Adherents of the resource-based view generally agree that the most strategically important resource is knowledge. A further important distinction has been drawn between tacit and explicit knowledge. Explicit knowledge can be coded in writing or symbols. This distinction between the two types of knowledge is important because of the transferability and appropriability of explicit knowledge, as opposed to tacit knowledge.

Tacit knowledge is acquired by and stored within individuals and cannot be transferred or traded as a separate entity. Explicit knowledge has the character of a public good. Two important consequences follow. First, tacit knowledge is a crucial source of sustainable competitive advantage because it is difficult for competitors to imitate it. Second, the contribution of a particular employee's tacit knowledge to a team output cannot be measured and paid accordingly. Following economists' advice to "run a firm as if it were a set of markets" means rewarding employees according to their marginal productivity and relying on extrinsic rather than intrinsic motivation.

Employees are extrinsically motivated if they are able to satisfy their needs indirectly, especially through monetary compensation. Money is a "goal which provides satisfaction independent of the actual activity itself". Extrinsically motivated coordination in firms is achieved by linking employees' monetary motives to the goals of the firm. The ideal incentive system is strict pay-for-performance. Although many economists admit the existence of intrinsic motivation,they leave it aside because it is difficult to analyse and control. Even if the assumption of opportunism is an "extreme caricature", opportunism as a "worst-case scenario" is a prudent consideration when designing institutional structures.

Transactions cost theory goes a step farther by assuming that individuals are opportunistic and seek self-interest with guile. Opportunism is a strong form ofextrinsic motivation when individuals are not constrained by any rules. In the transactions cost view, the task is to establish institutional settings that mitigate the hazards and costs of opportunistic behaviour. Motivation is intrinsic if an activity is undertaken for one's immediate need satisfaction. Intrinsic motivation "is valued for its own sake and appears to be self.sustained". Intrinsic motivation can be directed to the activity's flow, to a self-defined goal such as climbing a mountain, or to the obligations of personal and social identities.

The ideal incentive system is in the work content itself, which must be satisfactory and fulfilling for the employees. The behavioural view of organisation emphasizes intrinsic motivation. This approach has a long tradition in motivation-based organisation theory. Intrinsic motivation is also drawn upon by critics of transaction cost theory, as does the literature on psychological contracts. They emphasise intrinsic motivation in the form of identification with the firm's strategic goals, shared purposes, and the fulfillment of norms for its own sake.

Proponents of the behavioural view tend to look only at the positive aspects of intrinsic motivation. They consider intrinsic motivation to be an undisputed organisational advantage because it lowers transaction cost and raises trust and social capital. However, intrinsically motivated employees do not always work to the benefit of their employers. Thus, intrinsic motivation has both disadvantages and advantages.

Motivation is not a goal in itself but should serve to support a firm's goals. Enterprises are not interested in producing some kind of intrinsic motivation with their employees, say, the joy of stamp collecting. Rather, employees must be motivated to perform in a coordinated and goal oriented way. For this purpose, managers must compare the benefits and costs related to motivating employees intrinsically and extrinsically.

Two specific problems arise in connection with relying on intrinsic motivation in an organisation. First, changing intrinsic motivation is more difficult, and the outcome more uncertain, than relying on extrinsic motivation, or carrots and sticks. For this reason, economists as well as managers traditionally prefer a reward and command policy. Second, intrinsic motivation can have an undesirable content.

As history shows, some of the most terrible crimes have been motivated intrinsically, at least in part. Envy, vengeance, and the desire to dominate are not less intrinsically motivated than altruism, conscientiousness, and love. All of these motives contribute to immediate satisfaction rather than to achieving externally set goals. To discipline the effects of undesirable intrinsic motivation, external interventions via carrots and sticks are needed. Management makes unwanted outcomes of intrinsic motivation on coworkers, superiors, and customers costly and therefore less attractive.

In a careful analysis, Hirschman shows that uncontrolled passions are generally checked by economic interests. Montesquieu took as self-evident in his doctrine of "'doux commerce'" that "commerce improves and mitigates our behaviour as we can see every day." "Commerce," or external reward, makes extrinsic motivated behaviour easier to calculate than intrinsic motivation. Although intrinsic motivation has disadvantages, under specific conditions it is superior to extrinsic motivation in circumstances relevant for organisations. First, intrinsic motivation is needed for tasks that require creativity.

In contrast, extrinsically motivated persons tend to produce stereotyped repetition of what already works. In addition, experimental research shows that the speed of learning and conceptual understanding are reduced when people are monitored. With extrinsically motivated employees, therefore, the pressure of sanctions leads to lower learning levels and the work performed is more superficial than with intrinsically motivated employees. Second, intrinsic motivation also helps overcome the so-called multiple task problem, where contracts cannot completely specify all relevant aspects of employee behaviour and its desired outcome. Moreover, the goals to be set are often not clear to the principals.

Financial goals cannot always be broken down into operational goals for employees.Accordingly, contracts offering incentives to reach given goals can give rise to dysfunctional behavioural responses. Agents focus only on the rewarded aspects of the job and disregard the unrewarded ones. Nor do they have sufficient incentives to reflect on the adequacy of the goals they should achieve for the overall success of the firm. Multiple task problems are the subject of incomplete contracts, which are characteristic of employment contracts.

Empirical evidence suggests that the outcome of incomplete contracts will not normally be evaluated by variable pay-for-performance. Rather, firms rely considerably on intrinsic motivation. Finally, and most important, intrinsic motivation enables the generation and transfer of tacit knowledge under conditions in which extrinsic motivation fails. In these cases, the multiple task problem is combined with the problem of "free riding" in teams.

If the two types of motivation were independent and additive, intrinsic and extrinsic motivation could be managed by firms according to their relative advantages and disadvantages. The separation of intrinsic and extrinsic motivation would also correspond to a useful division of labor between psychology (focussing on intrinsic motivation) and economics (focussing on extrinsic incentives). However, a large number of careful experiments in psychology, as well as field research in economics, strongly suggest that under specific conditions there is a trade-off between the two types of motivation. The most important condition for this trade-off is the existence of intrinsic motivation in the first place.

In psychology, the trade-off has been called the "hidden costs of reward" or "the corruption effect of extrinsic motivation". In economics, Frey introduced the corruption effect as '"crowding-out." Many parents are intuitively aware of the corruption effect. Children who are initially enthusiastic about a task lose part of their interest when they are promised a reward for fulfilling the task. An example is the attempt to motivate children with rewards for doing their homework. In the short run, this measure is often successful.

In the longer run, however, the effect is that the children will do their homework only if.they receive a monetary reward. The crowding out effect has set in. Moreover a spill-over effect often occurs. The children don't do any housework except they are paid. Theoretical foundations for the crowding effect are based on cognitive evaluation theory and on psychological contract theory. These two psychological approaches have been developed largely independent of each other. Taken together, they specify the conditions under which intrinsic motivation is decreased or increased. These theories concentrate on preferences, i.e., attitudes referring to individuals.... structure of values. In contrast, traditional economists take values as constant and focus on constraints such as given prices, limited income, and time. The crowding theory acknowledges that observed behaviour depends on both preferences and constraints, relative prices in particular.

Cognitive Evaluation Theory

According to cognitive evaluation theory advanced by Deci, intrinsic motivation depends on the perceived locus of control. If the impetus for an action is attributed to an external influence, the perceived cognitive self-determination is undermined. Individuals who feel forced by outside intervention to behave in a specific way would be "overjustified" if they maintained their intrinsic motivation. The locus of control shifts from inside to outside the person. The actor attributes responsibility to the person undertaking the outside intervention.

A shift in the locus of control does not always take place. Each external intervention, e.g., a reward, has two aspects: a controlling and an informing aspect. The controlling aspect strengthens perceived external control and the feeling of being stressed from the outside. The informing aspect influences one's perceived competence and strengthens the feeling of internal control. Depending on which aspect is prominent, intrinsic motivation is reduced or raised.A positive effect on intrinsic motivation of an external intervention or institution is called crowding-in.

A negative effect is called crowding-out. If achieving a task is at the same time extrinsically and intrinsically motivated, the more devalued the attribution of a self-determined action is, the more strongly the individuals believe themselves to be subject to outside control. What matters is that when one goal is taken to be instrumental for reaching another goal, the first goal loses its value.

Social psychologists, as well as some unorthodox economists, suggest that contracts may involve strong emotional ties and loyalties. These socio-emotional relations establish an implicit contract that goes beyond transactional exchanges but include a reciprocal appreciation of intrinsic motivation. If such a contract is breached, the reciprocal good faith is put into question.

In this case, as empirical evidence shows, the parties to the contract perceive that the employment arrangement is transformed into an extrinsically motivated (transactional) contract. For example, when guests express their appreciation of a host's efforts with a symbolic gift (such as a bunch of flowers), the host's intrinsic motivation.tends to be raised. However, when guests try to present money as a gift, the host's intrinsic motivation is decreased.

An important part of psychological contracts involves perceptions of fairness. Experiments and field studies show that fairness increases the willingness to perform and decreases shirking. The reciprocal appreciation of motives also explains why commands normally crowd-out intrinsic motivation more than the use of prices. Commands do not take into account the motives of the recipients, while the price system leaves the choice open as to whether one cares to receive the reward or not.

Crowding Theory

Observed behaviour depends on preferences or intrinsic motivation (emphasised by psychologists) and on constraints or relative prices. Crowding theory considers both. External interventions, therefore, may have a positive or negative effect on work effort, depending on whether the effect on constraints or on preferences dominates. Fortunately, no less than five formal meta-analytical studies of the crowding theory have already been completed. Rummel and Feinberg used 45 experimental studies covering the period 1971 to 1985; Wiersma, 20 studies covering 1971 to 1990; and Tang and Hall, 50 studies from 1972 to 1992. These meta-analyses essentially support the.findings that intrinsic motivation is undermined if the externally applied rewards are perceived by the recipients to be controlling.

This view was challenged by Cameron and Pierce and Eisenberger and Cameron, who concluded that the undermining effect is largely "a myth" on the basis of their own meta-analysis of studies published in the period 1971 to 1991. These studies attracted a great deal of attention, and many scholars seem to have concluded that no such thing as a crowding-out effect exists. Deci, Koestner and Ryan identified a number of significant shortcomings and misinterpretations in Cameron and Pierce's analysis. Shortcomings include the omission of nearly 20 percent of the relevant studies as outliers; the use of mistaken control groups; and the misclassification of some of the studies.

In addition, Cameron and Pierce included dull and boring tasks for which a crowding-out effect could not occur, since the participants had no intrinsic motivation to begin with. To correct these failures, Deci, Koestner and Ryan (forthcoming) conducted an extensive meta-analysis including all the studies considered by Cameron, Pierce, and Eisenberger, as well as several studies that appeared after theirs.

It turns out that tangible rewards undermine intrinsic motivation for interesting tasks (i.e., tasks for which the experimental subjects show an intrinsic interest) in a highly significant and very reliable way and that the effect is moderately large. This undermining is particularly true for monetary compensations that were perceived by the experimental subjects to be controlling and therefore tended to crowd out intrinsic motivation. The crowding-out effect was stronger with monetary than with symbolic rewards.

The crowding-out effect was also larger with expected than with unexpected rewards. When the problems at issue were complicated, the negative relationship between reward and performance was stronger than when the problems were simple. In all cases, the behaviour was initially perceived to be interesting and therefore intrinsically rewarding. The relevance of the crowding-out effect is also supported by numerous field studies.

Another real-life case for the crowding-out effect is provided by blood donations, as argued by Titmuss. Paying donors for giving blood undermines the intrinsic motivation to do so. Though it is difficult to isolate the many different influences on blood supply, in countries where most of the blood is supplied gratis, paying for blood is likely to reduce total supply.

The crowding-out effect has also been shown to exist in econometric analyses for the so-called Not-In-My-Back-Yard syndrome, also know as NIMBY syndrome. In a carefully designed survey for a community located in central Switzerland, more than half the respondents (50.8 per cent) agreed to have a nuclear waste repository built in their commune. When compensation (in monetary terms) was offered, the level of acceptance dropped to 24.6 per cent.

Baumol and Oates, Hahn and Kelman observed that under certain conditions the introduction of environmental charges has little effect. When a punishment for environmental pollution is perceived to be strongly controlling, people are demotivated to protect the environment for intrinsic reasons. The crowding-in effect has been investigated less, but is supported by at least one econometric study.

A cross-section analysis of the 26 cantons in Switzerland with varying degrees of direct democratic institutions shows that in cantons with better developed institutions of direct democracy, citizens exhibit a higher intrinsic motivation to pay taxes than in those cantons with less participation rights.

Cantons with better developed democratic institutions are more informed and feel more fairly treated. Consequently they are less inclined to evade taxes. As pointed out, no crowding-out can take place if there is no intrinsic motivation in the first place. This condition obtains for simple jobs. In such cases, empirical evidence shows that the price effect increases performance. Lazear provides an empirical example. He finds that in a large auto glass company, productivity increases of between 20 percent to 36 percent of output were reached when the firm switched from paying hourly wages to piece rates.

Although general crowding effects have not been fully explored, we can still surmise the consequences of specific organisational designs on motivation. There are three aspects of crowding effects that should be taken into consideration when integrating market elements (such as profit centers or variable pay for performance) into the firm.

Participation is an alternative to markets as a coordination mechanism. Participation signifies an agreement on common goals. Participation raises the perceived self-determination of employees and therewith strengthens intrinsic motivation. This the strengthening of self-determination and intrinsic motivation takes place only when agreements about the goals serve primarily as self-control and self-obligation.

In contrast, perceived external control inhibits creativity in the pursuit of goals. These experimental findings support the concept of management by objectives as a process of joint goal setting between a principal and an agent. The recent emphasis on "empowerment" also reflects this relationship. Personal relationship in lieu of the anonymous market is a precondition for establishing psychological contracts based on emotional loyalties, often called team spirit.

Team-based structures enable such personal relationship. As experimental research shows, personal relationship strongly raises the intrinsic motivation to cooperate. These findings confirm that Likert's linking-pin-organisation as a network of interlocking teams indeed raises intrinsic motivation based on psychological.contracts. In contrast, neither perfect markets nor the price system rely on psychological contracts. An example is the anonymous relationship between buyers and sellers on financial markets.

Adam Smith was one of the first to recognise that the absence of personal relationship or social atomisation is a prerequisite for perfect competition. Contingency of reward on performance can crowd out intrinsic motivation. This holds provided the perceived controlling effect of reward is stronger than the perceived informing effect and the price effect is overruled. The crowding-out effect provides a possible interpretation for the overwhelming empirical evidence that there is generally no valid connection between pay and performance.

Instead, the "literature on incentive plans is full of vivid descriptions of the counterproductive behaviours that piece-rate incentive plans produce". The same holds for managerial compensation, a fact admitted even by the proponents of principal agent theory, who favor time-based compensation and oppose strict forms of variable pay-for-performance in situations that need high intrinsic motivation.

Managing motivation, especially balancing intrinsic and extrinsic motivation, is an important and hard-to-imitate competitive advantage. This capability is crucial for all tasks in which the goals are difficult to formulate and where it is difficult to attribute task completion to particular employees. As pointed out, the generation and transfer of knowledge often constitutes such a task. At the same time the generation and transfer of knowledge is the most crucial resource of firms.

Employees who are extrinsically motivated could resort to free riding. This situation cannot be alleviated by strengthening the carrot-and-stick policy when the conditions for crowding-out apply. In such conditions, external interventions undermine the needed intrinsic motivation of employees. However, managing intrinsic motivation is difficult and often risky. Situations that require intrinsic motivation must be distinguished from those that do not.

Markets rely systematically on price effects and therefore can crowd out the intrinsic motivation needed for specific forms of knowledge generation and transfer. The organisational forms that integrate market elements into firms with those not using market elements.

With the launch of its first personal computer in 1981, IBM chose to outsource all the major components. The microprocessor was bought from Intel, while the operating system was licensed from Microsoft. Moreover, the distribution channels were outsourced to a large number of retailers such as ComputerLand, Sears, BusinessLand, and MicroAge. The strong extrinsic incentives produced by the market enabled IBM to get its first PC to market in only 15 months and to launch an attack against Apple, the market pioneer.

However, with the passage of time, IBM had to learn a lesson. Because outsourcing necessitates making knowledge explicit to allow production and service level agreements, the competitors in the markets for PCs had an open door to imitate. They could buy the same operating system from Microsoft, the same software from Lotus, WordPerfect, and Microsoft and use the same distribution channels. As a result, IBM lost much of its competitive advantage as well as its ability to direct the evolution of the PC architecture.

However, the right balance between insourcing and outsourcing is crucial because no company is able to develop internally all the technology necessary for a successful future product. Chesbrough and Teece discuss Motorola, a leader in wireless communication technology, as a firm that has chosen the right balance. To retain its competitive advantage over the long run, battery technology is critical for Motorola. It therefore develops the critical parts of its value chain (fuel cells and solid-state energy sources) internally and buys the less critical battery technologies, such as nickel cadmium, on the market.

In situations of a marketable product or a contract, monetary rewards and extrinsic motivation fulfill their task.In the case of profit centers, transfer prices referring to comparable market prices serve to calculate the.contribution of each unit to the corporate outcome. Transfer prices help to remunerate leaders of profit centers according to their performance.But as the example of IBM shows, a problem arises when the resources become imitable,The very idea of extrinsically motivated competition between decentralised units hinders the flow of tacit knowledge to where it is needed.

Therefore the critical parts of the value chain should not be outsourced or separated into different profit centers. The exchange of tacit knowledge is concentrated within an organisational unit. In addition, knowledge remains tacit and cannot be translated into action subject to commands. Examples are the construction of complex facilities or the development of an outstanding product design like Benetton's fashion design.

The tacit knowledge is embodied in the product itself or in the firm-specific routinised processes leading to the product. Because of the tacitness of this knowledge, it can neither be made explicit via reverse engineering nor can it be encapsulated in an expert-system software. In the case of Benetton, fashion design moreover has to be integrated with garment knowledge, Benetton's own market knowledge, and its manufacturing expertise.

In team-based compensation, a crowding-in effect is produced if pay is accompanied by nonfinancial social recognition strengthening perceived competence. In any case, an intrinsic motivation to generate and transfer tacit knowledge cannot be compelled but can only be enabled under suitable conditions. By its nature, intrinsic motivation is always voluntary. The generation and transfer of explicit knowledge is not associated only with extrinsic motivation, nor does the transfer of tacit knowledge always require intrinsic motivation.

As Nonaka and Takeuchi show, the conversion of tacit into explicit knowledge at the individual level is an important part of the process of creating firm-specific tacit knowledge. During this process, individual tacit knowledge is amplified and crystallised in the form of routines. According to the resource-based view of the firm, organisational routines, embodied in the individual....s as well as in the firm....s tacit knowledge, are the most sustainable source of hard-to-imitate competitive advantages.

Nonaka and Takeuchi characterise the process of organisational knowledge creation as "knowledge spiral," in which tacit and explicit knowledge interact during four modes of knowledge conversion. In the socialisation mode, tacit knowledge is shared between individuals mainly as learning by doing. In the externalisation mode, parts of tacit knowledge are translated into explicit knowledge. Externalisation is supported by metaphors, analogies, narratives, or visuals.

In the combination mode, different explicit knowledge is bundled together, mainly by the exchange of documents, computerised communication, or formal education. Thus, the body of explicit knowledge becomes enriched and systemised. In the internalisation mode, the new body of explicit knowledge is conversed into rules of action and practice, i.e., the "firm....s memory" in the form of routines. Routines serve to enable the firm to deal with bounded rationality while at the same time acting as a repository of firm-specific knowledge.

To a high degree, routines are applied habitually and therefore become integrated into the body of tacit knowledge stored within individuals. At the same time, the habitually stored and practiced routines become integrated into the shared organisational tacit knowledge. The "knowledge spiral" turns around to a higher and richer level of shared knowledge. Thus, both socialisation and externalisation are required to create an ever growing body of organisational routines.

Externalisation as part of the process of creating firm-specific routines takes place in "knowledge producing teams." Examples are quality circles or task forces. Both are widely used to enhance total quality and continuous improvement in many industries, e.g., in car manufacturing. Participants contribute their mostly tacit knowledge about the production process by using e.g. narratives. The aim is to implement improved routines, which become part of the firm....s repository of knowledge.

Motivation in New Organisational Forms

During the last two decades, the infusion of market elements into hierarchies and the disaggregation of large corporations into autonomous molecular units has been the dominant recommendation for the restructuring of organisational forms to motivate firm members and coordinate their activities. Recently, more and more firms replace the strong emphasis on market-like governance arrangements in favour of a stronger centralisation and joint decision making. The present section reviews the motivational aspects within transaction cost economics and the knowledge-based view.

Existence of the firm

For many years, the theory of the firm was dominated by organisational economics. It seeks to answer the following two questions : "What is the purpose of firms?" and "what determines their scale and scope?". The knowledge-based view of the firm adds an additional question:

"why do firms differ and how does it matter?". By now, a major stream of research has investigated in detail the partially contradictory assumptions between the two approaches.

Although the property rights approach is also an important perspective in organisational economics, we focus on transaction cost economics. There are two reasons. Firstly, the property rights approach is less interested than transaction cost economics in different internal governance structures. Secondly, by emphasising incomplete contracting and residual decision rights, the strength of the property rights approach is that it clearly articulates the role of market incentives and how they can be altered by shifts in asset ownership. But the weakness is that it overlooks the great variety of incentive designs firms can use.

Transaction cost economics view

Transaction cost economics traces the existence of the firm to the thinking, planning and contracting cost that accompany any transaction. The existence of hierarchical firms results from a failure in market efficiency. Reasons for market failure involve the different transaction cost of negotiating, monitoring, and enforcing contracts. They include team production externalities, market power and information asymmetry.

In Williamson's view, the greater the level of uncertainty and of transaction specific investment in a transaction, the greater the threat that people act opportunistically. Fear of post-contractual hold-ups and ex post bargaining costs determine the ex ante investment decisions. Bringing a transaction from the market into the firm mitigates the hazards that accrue from opportunistic behaviour and improves investment incentives. The reason is that hierarchical forms of governance bring parties to an exchange under the direct control of a third party. This authoritative party monitors the behaviour of all parties involved. In transaction cost economics, the existence of firms is explained as resulting from incentive problems, especially opportunism.

Williamson does not claim that all members of an organisation act opportunistically, but it is prudent to consider the worst case of behaviour. Thus, opportunistic behaviour is introduced as an exogenously given assumption. Another important aspect of transaction cost economics concerns the distinction between production costs and transaction costs. By focusing on transactions as the basis unit of analysis, transaction cost economics regards economic exchange decisions as primary. The production functions of firms are assumed to be more or less identical, which allows scholars to focus on the allocation and exchange of goods and services. A shift from static to dynamic efficiency is not encompassed, as Williamson rightly concedes. Thinking in given choice sets, however, neglects the ability of a firm to foster innovation, learning and knowledge creating processes for new products.

Knowledge-based view

The knowledge-based view changes the perspective "from the historically dominant theme of value appropriation to the one of value creation" and focuses on the problem-solving dimensions of organisations. The notion of the firm is not seen as a bundle of transactions but as a firm-specific bundle of resources and the underlying processes therein. Those firms that control hard to imitate resources earn rents and gain a sustained competitive advantage that other firms find too costly to imitate. Distinctive skills, routines and knowledge are treated as the most important resources that establish a dynamic capability or a competence. Emphasis is thus placed on the firm's internal processes and production arrangements.

The knowledge-based view tends to neglect incentive issues. Although it does not deal with the assumption of opportunism and potentially conflicting interests, it is not determined why firm members should be willing to share and integrate their knowledge. Implicitly, this view implies an utopian view of "benevolent co-operators" who give up personal knowledge without adequate compensation.

As a consequence, the knowledge-based view contradicts the transaction cost view concerning the content of motivation. But in accordance with transaction costs economics, it introduces a given kind of motivation, in the one case benevolence, in the other case opportunism. Benevolence is a kind of intrinsic motivation in contrast to opportunism, which is a strong form of extrinsic motivation, where individuals are not constrained by any rules.

Extrinsic and intrinsic motivation

Extrinsic motivation occurs when employees are able to satisfy their needs indirectly, most importantly through monetary compensation. Money as such does not provide direct utility but serves to acquire desired goods and services, assumption which is basic to all economic analysis. Extrinsically motivated coordination in firms is achieved by linking employees' monetary motives to the goals of the firm. The preferred incentive system in economic theory is strict pay for performance.

Motivation is intrinsic if an activity is undertaken for the immediate satisfaction of one's needs. Intrinsic motivation "is valued for its own sake and appears to be self sustained". Intrinsic motivation can be directed

a) to the activity's flow – for example reading a novel,

b) to a self-defined goal – for example climbing a mountain, or

c) to the obligations of personal and social norms for their own sake, e.g. benevolence, identity, norms of distributive fairness and procedural fairness.

Intrinsic motivation is fostered by commitment to the work itself, which must be both satisfactory and fulfilling for the employees. It follows that "if you want people motivated to do a good job, give them a good job to do".

The existence of extrinsic and intrinsic motivation has important consequences for the problems created by social dilemmas and the incentive to invest in firm-specific pool resources. We will argue that firm-specific pool resources determine the main characteristics of firms in contrast to markets.

Firm-specific Pool Resources and Social Dilemmas

We use the term "firm-specific pool resources" to characterise goods (i) whose access is restricted to members of the firm in question, and (ii) firm members have open access. This leads to the problem that firm members may free ride on such resources of the firm. These resources are club goods in the sense of Buchanan. We use the term firm-specific pool resources instead of club goods because we want to link the public choice analysis of common pool resources with the analysis of dependence relations and complementarities in organisation theory. We emphasise the motivational aspects involved and use Ostrom's empirically based insights of how to overcome the free riding problems arising.

While Ostrom focuses on tangible common pool resources like fishing grounds and pastures with its concomitant problems of overuse, in firms intangible goods invite free riding resulting in undersupply of these firm specific resources. Examples are corporate culture, mutual commitment, common organisational rules and routines and accumulated firm specific knowledge, or absorptive capacity, as widely discussed within the knowledge-based theories of the firm. Intangible firm-specific are hard to codify in an easily verifiable and observable way whenever they are based to a large extent on tacit knowledge.

Today, organisational knowledge is seen to be the most important intangible firm-specific pool resource. It can be thought of as the "feed stock" of competences and capabilities. Most scholars agree that common tacit knowledge is the resource most difficult to imitate. Therefore, this is the most important source of sustainable competitive advantage. Tacit knowledge is partly idiosyncratic and therefore necessarily creates a situation of asymmetric information.

The output of individuals' tacit knowledge, e.g. of an individual salesperson, can be measured. In contrast, a specialist's contribution of tacit knowledge to a good or service produced by a team can hardly be evaluated either by looking at outputs or inputs. This holds both for a principal outside the team and for team members. An example is the Benetton's fashion designing team. If a mainly extrinsically motivated person cannot be excluded from obtaining the benefits of a collective product or service once it is produced, he or she has little incentive to contribute voluntarily to the joint effort, but free-rides on the efforts of others. If all firm members choose to free-ride, the firm-specific pool resources will not be produced. Thus, there is an immediate danger that intangible firm-specific pool resources are undersupplied. A social dilemma arises.

The advantage of hierarchies over markets derives from obtaining joint benefits if firm members are motivated to invest in firm-specific pool resources. The accumulation of this pool cannot be brought about by external incentives or a particular property rights allocation. In this situation, a social dilemma is imminent. Miller even claims it to be at the heart of the managerial problem. Social dilemmas arise in situations in which individuals are interdependent with respect to valuable but potentially intangible firm-specific pool resources.

In response to such interdependence, firm members have to choose whether they follow a competitive course of action that furthers their own interests at the expense of others, or contribute to a cooperative solution that furthers joint interests. If firm members realise that their own efforts to invest in pool resources will have little impact if others do not do likewise, they have little incentive to cooperate themselves. There is a trade-off between self-interest - where each firm member receives a larger individual "pay-off" by not contributing - and social efficiency - where all firm members are better off if everyone decides to cooperate.

The traditional solutions to the prisoners' dilemma are hierarchical authority, the "visible hand" and in political economy, the Leviathan. Although these solutions provide the unity and coherence needed in a firm, they seem to fail whenever there is high information asymmetry. This is especially true whenever tacit knowledge is highly important. It follows that firms not only exists because of transaction cost reasons. They exist because "they provide a social community of voluntaristic action structured by organising principles that are not reducible to individuals". This supports the creation of value when individual inputs or outputs are not observable and measurable. How do the two approaches, the knowledge-based view and transaction cost economics, deal with the problem of social dilemmas and the incentives to invest in firm-specific pool resources?

Knowledge-based view

Within the knowledge-based view, the major theme is the generation of dynamic capabilities as the most important intangible firm-specific pool resources. Firms function on the basis of organisational and cultural rules, informal relations and tacit norms. These are knowledge assets that are based on firm-specificity, social complexity and causal ambiguity, which cannot be reduced to individual skills. They are assembled in integrated clusters spanning firm members so that cooperation and coordination is achieved.

This approach, however, does not realise social dilemmas as a problem. It is implicitly assumed that no conflicts of interest exist. Firm members engage voluntarily in a course of collective action and contribute to firm-specific pool resources that can only be generated in the body of an organised group of individuals. But the assumption of no interest conflicts is problematic: selfish individuals want to maintain their monopolistic position as holders of idiosyncratic knowledge. Because tacit knowledge is not contractible, they would not share it with others voluntarily. Thus, the knowledgebased view takes non-self-interested intra-firm commitment to cooperate implicitly for granted, while (external) incentive issues do not really matter.

Transaction cost economics

In contrast, transaction cost economics acknowledges the existence of social dilemmas. It is presumed that those dilemmas can be solved through monitoring and sanctioning arrangements. Without monitoring, selfish employees do not contribute to the generation of firm-specific assets which include firm-specific pool resources. According to this view, organisations can solve problems of opportunism in a manner that is more efficient than market mechanisms. In transaction cost economics, the main attributes that describe a mode of governance are incentive intensity, administrative control and legal rules regime. The burden of investing in the arrangements necessary to organise collective action is undertaken by one individual (the entrepreneur), whose returns are directly related to the surplus generated. Consequently, the entrepreneur's threats to punish are credible.

Still, it is highly questionable whether social dilemmas can be solved in this way. In transaction cost economics, the solution of social dilemmas does not pose a problem, because the exchange of goods and services, including the transfer of knowledge, are regarded as potentially contractible. This means in principle that they can be measured in isolation and can clearly be controlled. However, this is not possible for intangible pool resources, like tacit knowledge in teams. Investing in those resources is not observable and not verifiable. Free-riding can take place. Innovations in measurement, stemming from improvements in information technology, cost accounting, or benchmarking, do not solve the dilemma.

Some authors, who recognise these problems, try to offer another solution: they argue that repeated games of "relational contracts" may provide a cooperative outcome to social dilemma situations, that is agreements enforced by the firm members' concern for their reputations. If a firm member's contribution to firm-specific pool resources is too complex and subtle to be verified by a monitor, subjective performance assessments can be used by managers who are well placed to observe these subtleties (e.g. excessive overtime or punctuality) of the firm members' behaviour and opportunities. However, this tends to induce inefficient behavioural responses. The non-verifying nature of these measures gives rise to the possibility that their true values will be manipulated or distorted.

For these reasons, we go along with Hardin: the social dilemma has no technical solution. In this sense, social dilemmas are a problem of managing motivation and not a problem of precise measuring and monitoring. Conceptualising a firm as a commons draws attention to the question of how firms can induce the right kind of cooperation – the motivation of their members to share their knowledge and to deviate from self-interested behaviour.

Dynamics of Motivation in the Firm

Introducing the dynamics between extrinsic and intrinsic motivation helps to determine which factors influence the intensity and quality of the production of intangible firm-specific pool resources, especially tacit knowledge. How can firms induce an efficient kind of cooperation – the motivation of their members to share their knowledge and deviate from self-interested behaviour – when the price system and monitoring fail? An important part of the answer to this question relates to motivational factors concerning crowding effects.

Crowding effects

Overwhelming theoretical and empirical evidence exists that intrinsic and extrinsic motivation are not additive as standard economics assume. Rather, there is a systematic dynamic relationship between the two. This dependence has been shown to exist in a large number of careful experiments undertaken in psychology by Deci and his group, as well as in field research in economics. The relationships between intrinsic and extrinsic motivation are called crowding effects. These effects make both kinds of motivation endogenous variables.

Crowding effects can be subdivided into a crowding-out- and a crowding-in-effect. The crowding-out-effect posits a negative relationship between intrinsic and extrinsic motivation. When external incentives - rewards or commands – are perceived to be controlling by the firm member affected, intrinsic motivation tends to be undermined. In particular, firm members' work morale may be reduced when they receive monetary incentives that are contingent on their performance ("pay for performance"). Crowdingout can take place only if there was a significant amount of intrinsic motivation in the first place.

The crowding-in-effect posits a positive relationship between intrinsic and extrinsic motivation. Outside intervention in the form of rewards or commands may strengthen intrinsic motivation if it is perceived to be supportive of intrinsic motivation. Thus, a pay rise or another external incentive may in certain circumstances be considered to reflect an appreciation of one's work by superiors and therefore tends to increase work morale.

Theoretical foundations for the crowding effects are based on cognitive evaluation theory and on psychological contract theory. According to cognitive evaluation theory, external intervention may reduce selfdetermination. When people perceive external intervention as a restriction to acting autonomously, intrinsic motivation is substituted by these external interventions. The locus of control shifts from inside to outside the person.

According to psychological contract theory, reciprocity can be violated. The implicit contract based on mutual acknowledgement of one's engagement is violated when a task undertaken by intrinsic motivation is rewarded extrinsically. Conversely, maintaining norms of reciprocity causes a higher willingness to perform and reduces shirking work.

Balancing intrinsic and extrinsic motivation

Motivation has to be managed so that the required intrinsic motivation is not crowded out. In particular, strong monitoring, pressure of sanctions, high-powered incentives as piece rates, bonuses, or other forms of variable pay for performance undermine firm members' work ethics. This holds in particular for complex jobs, where intrinsic motivation is necessary to contribute to intangible firm-specific pool resources. We focus on four aspects that firms have at their disposal for enabling motivation and regulating conflict.

Participation is directed to an agreement on common goals. If this agreement primarily serves as self-control and self-obligation, participation raises the perceived self-determination of employees. Therewith, it strengthens intrinsic motivation. Self organising principles enable the willingness to conform to social norms for their own sake. In this sense, they can foster the coordination for cooperative interactions of the divergent interests of different firm members.

Personal relationship is a precondition for establishing psychological contracts based on emotional loyalties, often called team spirit. Team-based structures enable such a personal relationship. As experimental research shows, personal relationships strongly raise the intrinsic motivation to cooperate.

Contingency of reward on performance can crowd out intrinsic motivation. This holds provided the perceived controlling effect of reward is stronger than the perceived informing effect and the price effect is overruled. Thus, the crowding-out-effect provides a possible explanation for the empirical evidence suggesting that there is generally no significant connection between pay and performance, except for simple jobs.

REFERENCES

Amabile, T. M. (1983). The social psychology of creativity: A componential conceptualization. *Journal of Personality and Social Psychology,* 45, 357-376.

Hersey, P. and K.H. Blanchard (1982) *Management of Organisational Behaviour; utilizing Human Resources.* 4th Edition. Prentice Hall of India Pvt. Ltd. New Delhi 110 001. P. 343.

Kolb, D.A., I.M.. Rubin and J.M. Mc Intyre (1979) *Organizational Psychology – an experiential approach.* Third edition Prentice-Hall, INC., Englewood cliffs, New Jersey 07632. P. 496.

8

Stress in Workplace

We hear a lot about stress. People talk about being stressed out, how this or that situation is stressful. Stress affects us at home, work, and even on holidays. We also hear too often that we should learn to "deal" or "cope" with stress at work. This implies that workplace stress is normal and that we need to "manage" or "handle" stress and just get on with the job. This view of stress is wrong. Workplace stress is a serious health and safety hazard that can have devastating effects. Stress can lead to psychosocial illnesses, such as anxiety and depression.

While it is true that there are sources of stress other than the workplace, this does not mean that workplace stress is not a hazard or that it is the product of a worker's imagination. Reorganisation, layoffs, job insecurity, accelerated paces of work, along with many physical work hazards can all contribute to stress. These causes of stress are all firmly rooted in the workplace. Also, stress that is experienced outside of work for example within the family often has a workplace component to it, or is in some way caused by workplace factors.

This guideline is focused on workplace stress – stress that is caused by and comes from the workplace. The word "stress" is used with the phrase "workplace stress" almost interchangeably, but it is used mostly as a more general term. Stress is closely related to control. Many workplaces have changed, resulting in less control for members to direct their work. Less or low control over job tasks is associated with high stress levels.

This chapter outlines the scope of the stress problem as it affects CUPE members, assessing the issue, the causes, who is affected, and the hazards.

WHAT IS STRESS?

We know when we feel stress or stressed. It might seem the concept doesn't need to be defined. It is also true that stress can affect people differently.

But part of the hurdle of addressing stress as a health and safety issue is to define the hazard:

> Stress is a combination of physical and psychological reactions to events that challenge or threaten us. In normal circumstances, the stress response is a powerful protective mechanism that allows us to deal with sudden changes, dangers or immediate demands. In abnormal circumstances, stress overwhelms our protective mechanisms, leading to serious negative health outcomes.

This definition makes a key point that stress is often a result of combined factors – both physical and psychological.

According to this definition, stress occurs when there is a poor match between workplace demands and a worker's degree of control. We feel stress as a result of demands that are placed upon the mind and the body.

Stress: A Health and Safety Hazard

Stress is a health and safety hazard plain and simple. Employers might like to believe that stress does not exist. They might argue that stress is "in your imagination," a "personal problem" or a result of workers' "lifestyle choices." Or they might regard stress as just part of the job.

Like violence and overwork, stress is a significant health and safety hazard directly related to how work is organised. Workplace stress comes from how work is done. Because workplace stress affects workers' health, it must be seen as a workplace hazard and as a health and safety issue.

Normal and Toxic Stress

The first definition used earlier describes normal circumstances for stress: stress is dealt with and then it passes. Our instinctive reaction to stress is to combat or flee the source of stress known as the fight or flight reaction.

With normal stress we can fight or flee. The response occurs fairly quickly and then the stress ends. The three phases of normal stress are:

— Stress comes

— Stress goes

— Stress is over

— An example of normal stress is short-term anxiety because you have lost something important, or feeling temporarily stressed because your bus is stuck in traffic and you are late for work. When the item is found, or the bus gets you to work on time, your stress drops away and is eliminated. There are many day-to-day occurrences like these that cause normal stress.

Toxic stress is another matter. As the name suggests, toxic stress is like a poison. This form causes the most damage, as the human body is not equipped to deal with toxic stress. Unlike normal stress that comes and goes, toxic stress stays with you, building up the harmful effects. The three phases of toxic stress are:

— Stress comes

— Stress stays with you

— Stress builds up

Workers can experience toxic stress when they are exposed to staff shortages, harassment, bullying, noise, and other hazards. This form of stress often leads to negative physical and psychosocial effects.

Physical Reactions to Stress

Both normal and toxic stress affect the body physically, but toxic stress effects are more severe.

The Generalised Stress Response is the phrase used to describe a variety of physical reactions to stress, such as:

— An increased metabolism, for example, faster heartbeat and quicker breathing.
— Increased blood pressure.
— Increased cholesterol and fatty acids in the bloodstream.
— Decreased protein synthesis, impaired digestion and immune and allergic response systems.
— Faster blood clotting.
— Increased production of stomach acids.
— Increased production of blood sugar for energy.
— Localised inflammation
— Widened airways directing more oxygen into the muscles.
— Tensed up muscles.
— Increased sweating to cool muscles.

Stress can also cause workers to experience sensations such as a dry mouth and difficulty swallowing, shortness of breath, a racing heart, butterflies or knots in the stomach, and tension, aching, shaking, or pain in the muscles.

These physical reactions are immediate, instinctive responses to stressors. Over time, as these reactions occur too often – as normal stress progresses to toxic stress – it can translate into more severe physical and/or psychological effects, such as:

— Sleep disruption and disorders.
— Fatigue, apathy and lack of energy.
— Chronic aches and pains in the chest, shoulders, back, neck and elsewhere in the body.
— Depression and a general decrease in enjoyment of life.
— Changes in sexual activity.
— Conflict with family, friends, and co-workers.
— Weight gain or weight loss.
— Greater susceptibility to injury.
— Immune system depression, greater vulnerability to illness and disease.

— Other stress-related health problems, such as, ulcers, heart disease, headaches, irritable bowel syndrome, diabetes, and menstrual disorders.

Any combination of these effects can be very harmful to a worker's health and well-being.

Stress Myths and Clichés

Here is a quick look at some of the misinformation about stress. Don't be misled by employers and consultants who use phrases and make claims such as these:

— Stress is not a workplace health and safety hazard.

— A little bit of stress is healthy.

— Stress is good for you; it makes you more productive at your job.

— Stress comes from your home life, not the job.

— All we need to do is learn to cope with our stress.

— To deal with stress, all workers need to do is take a stress management course.

— Stress can be solved with exercise, breathing deeply and learning to relax more.

— Workplace wellness programs are the answer to stress.

— Here are the realities – key points to remember about stress:

— Stress is a health and safety hazard.

— Stress can have serious health effects.

— On-the-job stressors cause workplace stress.

— Stress is largely caused by poor workplace organisation.

— Your joint health and safety committee should deal with stress hazards.

— Workers need control over their jobs to eliminate stress.

Be wary of employers who claim stress is normal and unavoidable. Also be sceptical of employers who claim stress problems can be solved with stress management schemes, wellness programs, team-building exercises, and anything else that sounds warm and fussy. Stress management techniques only deal with the symptoms of workplace stress. They do not get rid of stressors. These programs do not prevent injuries or diseases. They are not a solution to workplace stress.

Relaxation techniques, counselling and coping mechanisms offer only temporary relief from stress. Workplace stress hazards must be dealt with at their source through primary prevention – not after the fact. Preventing exposure to the causes of stress is the only way to eliminate the hazard.

What Causes Stress?

Stressors cause stress. But what are these stressors and how do we pinpoint them? Here are a few causes of stress identified:

- Lack of training and direction.
- Too many demands at one time.
- Deadline pressures.
- Uncertainty.
- Office politics and hostile management.
- Stale air, either too hot or too cold.
- Lack of windows and natural lighting.
- Violence, threats and bullying.
- Too many bosses.
- Surveillance cameras.
- Working alone.
- Low morale among workers.
- Risk of injury and disease.

Work Organisation, Lack of Control and Excessive Demands

Work organisation factors cause stress or make stress worse. How jobs are designed, carried out, and the degree to which workers participate in the decision-making process at their workplace can result in stress.

The National Institute for Occupational Safety and Health (NIOSH) in the United States defines work organisation as the "work process and the organisational practices that influence job design." These are important elements as they can affect new work organisational practices. For example, if the country is going through tough economic times, this can lead to layoffs, cutbacks and downsising.

The following are among the many work organisation factors that can cause stress:

— Lack of control and conflicting work demands.
— Lack of participation in decision-making and lack of autonomy at work.
— Lack of training and direction, and changes in work organisation.
— Lack of recognition of work done and lack of respect from supervisors.
— Repetitive, boring and meaningless work.
— Unclear and conflicting work responsibilities.
— Low pay, lack of career development opportunities and job instability.
— Too much or too little work, overwork or under-use of skills.
— Poor communication, new technologies and time pressures.
— Privatisation, outsourcing, downsising, mergers, staff cutbacks, restructuring, and other large-scale work reorganisation schemes.
— Repressive management styles and techniques, such as Total Quality Management, constant improvement, teamworking, and quality circles.

Control is a central work organisation factor linked to stress. Lack of control at work can make workers sick. A lot of workplace stress research has focused on control and demand factors and how these lead to stress. Complicated models have been put forward to predict workers' stress levels, using terms like demand/control/support model, decision-making latitude and job strain hypothesis.

Lack of control is a cause of stress. It comes from not having the ability to decide how a job is done. Examples include not being able to decide the pace of work, or what tasks get done in what order.

Control is different from power. Control concerns factors within the job – how the job and its tasks are carried out. Power is broader than control and concerns decisions such as when work is scheduled, whether a worker will have or retain a job, which workers will get advancement within an organisation, and other larger scale decisions. Uncertainty over these broader power factors can also cause stress.

The control/demand model adds another factor. If workers have excessive demands placed upon them, they will suffer stress.

When lack of control is combined with high demands, a worker will almost certainly suffer high stress levels. These factors can create toxic workplace stress, causing increased heart disease and possibly death, depression, exhaustion, low self-esteem, and increased upper extremity musculoskeletal disorders. Job uncertainty can compound lack of control and high demands, making stress an even greater hazard.

Work organisation schemes, such as Total Quality Management (TQM) and quality circles might be introduced to workplaces and sold as a way for workers to gain more control over their work. After years of these practices being imposed on CUPE members and other workers, the opposite effect has emerged workers have less control. A recent NIOSH study of work reorganisation found that:

In 2001, the Communications Workers Union (CWU) in the United Kingdom surveyed 2,729 of its members about stress. CWU members were asked to rank causes of stress in order of importance. These workers ranked bad management, excessive workloads, staff shortages, and other poor work organisation factors as the leading causes of stress. Work organisation factors are the single biggest predictors of stress at work.

Overwork and Work Shift Schedules

Stress is among the many negative health effects caused by overwork and accelerated paces of work. Overwork — like stress — is a work organisation health and safety issue. It is characterised by:

— Long and difficult hours.

— Unreasonable work demands.

— Multi-tasking.

— Pressure to work overtime.

— Fewer rest breaks, days off, holidays and vacation.

— Faster, more pressured work pace.

— Performance monitoring.
— Unrealistic management expectations.
— Additional, often inappropriate, tasks piled on top of "core" duties
— No replacement during sick leave, holidays and vacations.

Overwork affects our quality of work. When workers can't get the job done the way they want it done, they will experience stress. In overwork conditions, the protective mechanism of the stress response breaks down due to fatigue, overexertion and other factors. These two health and safety hazards are both consequences of poor work organisation.

Long hours, shift work, and night work are stressors related to overwork. These stressors can disrupt workers' family and social life, increase fatigue, create sleep deficits, affect concentration, increase exposure to chemical hazards, and make workers more susceptible to workplace injuries and illnesses. All of these factors can also contribute to higher stress levels.

Part-time, casual, reduced-hours, temporary and split shift work can also cause stress. Part-time and reduced-hours workers suffer stress from not having enough hours to support themselves and irregular work shifts. Short notice for fulfilling work commitments can create stress for casual and temporary workers.

Physical Working Conditions

Physical work conditions can also be stressors, such as:

— Noise and vibration.
— Poor and inadequate lighting.
— Temperature extremes – too hot or too cold, or too much variation in temperature.
— Overcrowding, poor spacing and work area layout.
— Exposure to toxic substances.
— Ill-fitting and poorly designed work tools, furniture and workspaces.
— Poorly maintained work environment.

— Poor indoor air quality.
— Bad building design.
— Working with hazardous equipment.
— Lack of outside amenities and bad site planning – such as no parking, no access to public transit, no proximity to green space and recreational facilities.

Any of the above can cause or compound stress. Many of these stressors are also linked to work organisation. Other physical factors, such as the absence of windows and natural light in a workplace, have likewise been linked to higher stress levels for workers.

Job Insecurity, Cutbacks and Reorganisation

Workplaces have changed in recent years. Cutbacks, privatisation, reorgs, and downsising have contributed to a heightened sense of job insecurity. All of these factors are causes of workplace stress.

In two decades, public sector jobs dropped from one-fifth of all employment in Canada, to less than one sixth by 1996. The most severe cutbacks occurred between 1992-1996 when 121,000 jobs across the country were lost. During those same years, 694,000 jobs were created in the private sector and 266,000 more people opted for self-employment. These numbers represent huge cutbacks and downsising in the public sector, along with a massive shift towards privatisation. At the same time, public needs and expectations have not decreased. If anything, they have become greater.

Bullying, Harassment and Violence

These hazards can cause stress and are again linked to work organisation. Bullying has become a more widely-recognised hazard in Canadian workplaces. The British public sector trade union UNISON defines bullying as:

> Offensive, intimidating, malicious, insulting or humiliating behaviour, abuse of power or authority which attempts to undermine an individual or group of employees and which may cause them to suffer stress.

Bullying can create a dangerous, debilitating and negative workplace climate that elevates workers' stress levels. As a result, workers may suffer headaches, back pain, stomach ailments, insomnia, depression, fatigue, anxiety and even suicidal thoughts.

Harassment verbal abuse; threats; slurs; insults; discrimination on the basis of age, race, ethnic origin, gender, sexual orientation or ability; and its other forms — causes stress.

Progressive amendments to Quebec's Act Respecting Labor Standards and other Legislative Provisions in 2002 have added language on psychological harassment. It defines psychological harassment as:

> Any vexatious behaviour in the form of repeated and hostile or unwanted conduct, verbal comments, actions, or gestures, that affects an employee's dignity or psychological or physical integrity and that results in a harmful work environment for the employee.

The amendment to the province's legislation further states: "every employee has a right to a work environment free from psychological harassment."

Harassment reduces job satisfaction, can increase turnover at workplaces, and, like bullying, creates a workplace climate hazardous to workers' health and safety. Harassment is also linked to physical symptoms, such as stomach ailments, headaches, nausea, over and under eating, sexual problems, and deteriorated interpersonal relations.

Who is Affected by Stress?

Stress has been near the top of the health and safety priorities. The public sector in Canada has been damaged by cutbacks, privatisation schemes, and other initiatives. The result: high levels of stress for public sector workers.

A 2001 Canadian Policy Research Networks (CPRN) study found workplace stress had doubled. Twenty-seven percent of workers in 2001 compared to 13 percent of workers ten years earlier reported high job stress. As stress levels increased in Canadian workplaces, job satisfaction declined – the two seem to go hand-in-hand.

Women experience more stress than men, according to the CPRN study. Sixty-two percent of female non-professional workers and 59 percent of female professional workers reported high-perceived stress levels, compared to 54 percent of male non-professional workers and 43 percent of male professional workers. Female workers also reported higher levels of role overload.

These numbers do not indicate a weakness on women's part. Their stress levels are higher because women, more than men, generally have greater family responsibilities. Women still handle more childcare, child-raising, elder care and other family duties than men.

WHAT ARE THE STRESS PUTCOMES?

Stress can cause many negative health outcomes. CUPE members listed these effects of workplace stress:

— Headaches and tension.
— Chest and stomach pains.
— Joint and muscle pains; arthritis.
— Increased use of alcohol and drugs.
— Lower interest in sex.
— Feeling angry and aggressive more often.
— Weight gain and weight loss.
— Feeling antisocial and idle.

Psychological Disease and Social and Behavioural Changes

Stress is a known cause of many psychological diseases and disorders, as well as many social and behavioural changes, such as:

— Depression, feelings of apathy and low self-worth, crying spells.
— Anxiety, increased tension, fearfulness.
— Changes in eating habits.
— Sleep disorders, insomnia, fatigue and exhaustion.
— Irritability, mood changes, constant negativity, over-reaction and irrational behaviour.

— Inability to concentrate and see tasks through to their conclusion.

— Burnout.

— Sexual dysfunction.

— Increased use of drugs, alcohol and tobacco.

— Paranoia and social isolation and withdrawal.

— Suicidal thoughts.

Many of these outcomes can severely affect workers' lives. Descent into acute depression, for example, can cause workers to be off the job for years and end careers prematurely.

Specific worker studies have connected stress and psychological diseases. For example, high job demands among male power-plant workers have been associated with depressive disorders. Depression has also been linked with specific workplace stressors such as lack of job satisfaction, workplace role conflict and ambiguity.

Heart Disease and Other Physiological Outcomes

Exposure to job stress increases the risk of heart disease and other physiological problems. The physiological reactions to stress described earlier with the Generalised Stress Response can be early triggers of more severe heart problems to come.

Heart disease is the leading cause of death in Canada. It includes coronary heart disease, hypertensive disease, heart and circulatory system disorders, and other conditions. Stress in the workplace has been directly linked to many of these diseases. This can increase the possibility of heart attack. Stress can also upset the heart's cardiac rhythm. An excessively raised heartbeat can lead to life-threatening ventricular fibrillation. Numerous worker studies correlate stress and higher rates of heart disease.

Stress can also make workers vulnerable to other diseases, including:

— High blood pressure.

— Headaches and migraines.

— Impaired digestion – due to a decrease in intestinal movement.

— Menstrual disorders – there is some evidence of an association with stress.
— Ulcers – from lowered blood flow.
— Irritable bowel syndrome – there is some evidence of a link with stress.
— Diabetes – from excessive levels of fats and glucose released into the bloodstream.
— Various illnesses – from lowered immune function due to stress.

Personal and Family-life Conflict

Like any workplace hazard, the effects of stress can spill over from work and have an impact on workers' lives with their family and friends. With stress – especially with toxic stress – workers continue to suffer outside their working hours. Family and personal relationships suffer. Stress can contribute to exhaustion and fatigue, causing workers to lose interest in or feel too tired for personal or family hobbies and recreational activities. This can intensify the negative effects of stress, creating a vicious circle.

Striking a balance between work and life/family can be an impossible task. Juggling childcare arrangements, sick family members, elder care, and extended family responsibilities are difficult on their own. Workers' and their families' well-being are typically what suffer most.

Workers Divided

Stress can create conflict in the workplace that shows up as anger, frustration, envy and mistrust. Co-workers, stewards, staff representatives, and other union workers might become targets. Conflict can isolate workers from one another.

These circumstances divide workers and harm union solidarity. It is vital to understand that workplace stressors – such as how work is organised by your employer – cause the stress, not co-workers or the union. Don't let employer techniques such as performance monitoring and surveillance devices create competition and resentment. In a divided workplace, the employer gains and workers lose. When confronted by stress hazards, members need to remember that solutions and strategies for change depend on worker solidarity.

Work-related Musculoskeletal Disorders

Stress can contribute to work-related musculoskeletal disorders (WRMDs), also known as Repetitive Strain Injuries (RSI) and Musculoskeletal Injuries (MSI). WRMD is a catchall phrase for various injuries. These injuries usually involve repeated trauma to muscles, tendons, and peripheral nerves.

WRMDs have a work organisation component. Ergonomic injuries do not only result from manual working techniques, for example, how a worker holds a mop when mopping, or how a worker lifts materials.

Specific stress risk factors that have been linked to WRMDs include:

— Job dissatisfaction.

— Intensified workload.

— Monotonous and repetitive work.

— Low job control.

— Role uncertainty.

— Inadequate work-rest cycles.

— Limited social support from supervisors.

Workers are more vulnerable to WRMDs when suffering specific physiological reactions to stress. For example, stressors activate the central nervous system, which in turn increases muscle tone.

WRMDs. Stressors stimulate the autonomic nervous system, triggering the release of adrenalin and noradrenalin. Muscles and tendons then tighten, reducing the flow of nutrients to the tendons. These tendons will not self-heal if there are microlesions to the tendon fibres caused by ergonomic strain. The result: chronic muscle fatigue and muscle pain. An activated central nervous system can also cause corticosteroids to be released. This has been linked to tunnel syndromes.

Burnout

Working under continually stressful conditions can lead to burnout — the end result of physical and mental exhaustion caused by exposure to toxic stressors.

Some symptoms of burnout are:

- Emotional exhaustion, feeling emotionally overextended and nearly depleted of emotional resources.
- Negative feelings, irritability, and a deteriorated sense of self-image.
- A decline in feelings of competence and a decrease in work performance, feeling helpless and hopeless.
- Specific workplace stressors that cause burnout include role conflict at work, lack of control over one's job, and lack of social support on the job. Sufferers of burnout can be ill and away from work for long periods. They often withdraw from day-to-day life. Unlike depression, which can have many causes, burnout is directly linked to stressors at work

Synergistic Effects of Stress and Other Diseases

The effects of stress can work synergistically, combining with other illnesses and diseases to make worse those illnesses and diseases. An American study showed that workers who suffered toxic stress levels at work were three to five times more likely to catch a cold. Their stress levels made them more vulnerable to viral infection. In Finland, researchers studied the synergistic effects of stress and heart disease among manufacturing sector workers. A study of telecommunications workers looking at ergonomic injuries found higher rates of upper extremity musculoskeletal disorders among those with high stress levels caused by job pressures and low decision-making control at work. If workers suffer the effects of stress, they are at greater risk of other illnesses and injuries.

Critical Incident Stress

This condition – sometimes known as post-traumatic stress – can occur when workers are exposed to a single, severely stressful circumstance, such as a natural disaster, road accident, murder or assault.Critical incident stress is a serious condition that requires professional treatment and care. It is a serious health and safety hazard that must be prevented. In workplaces where there is the chance of critical incident stress affecting workers, programs to respond to workers' needs must be in place. Critical incident stress is beyond the scope of this guideline, which focuses on normal and toxic stress.

Is Stress A Health and Safety Hazard for You?

Stress is sometimes not regarded as an obvious health and safety hazard. On the surface, stress may not seem as direct a threat as asbestos, infectious diseases, or needlestick injuries. With those hazards, the threat is more clearly identifiable and the negative health outcomes are well documented and direct. Stress is not as cut and dry. It is related to work organisation issues and their outcomes. These outcomes might be attributed to some cause other than job insecurity. Burnout or anxiety is often dismissed as being caused by an individual's lifestyle or their "inability to cope." That incorrectly shifts blame to the worker instead of their workplace – a classic employer manoeuvre.

Identify the Problem

Many of us know that stress is what's causing our health, job satisfaction, morale, family and personal relationships to deteriorate.

Surveys and Questionnaires

Surveys usually involve handing out a written questionnaire. It's a great tool for gauging the extent of a health and safety issue. A sample stress questionnaire is provided at the end of this guideline. It can be used in full or in part.

Often the employer claims that there is no evidence for a problem like stress. When members can show the results from a questionnaire, they take a major step towards addressing stress by gaining recognition for the hazard.

It's a good idea to have either the union, through its health and safety committee, or the joint (union/management) health and safety committee involved. Prior to distributing the survey, hold some type of membership information session.

Any survey or questionnaire must be clear, concise and basic. It may be necessary for the local to have the questionnaire translated, taking into account dominant first languages among members in their workplace.

To a void any hassles later regarding the legitimacy of the process and results, the joint health and safety committee and/or the employer should approve the questionnaire.

Once the survey is ready, it should be distributed throughout the workplace. The union representatives on the joint health and safety committee should be responsible for collecting completed questionnaires.

There needs to be a plan and process in place for tabulating the questionnaires that are agreed to by those involved. Once the results are calculated, they should be presented and discussed at a union meeting, highlighting those issues that are central to stress in your workplace.

The results of the questionnaire need to be acted upon. It is not enough to just take the pulse of the membership. The questionnaire must form the basis for action by the joint health and safety committee to find solutions to workplace stress hazards.

If the employer or management representatives on the joint committee do not want to cooperate with conducting a survey, the union should survey the membership on its own. Similar procedures to those already described should be followed. However, the level of cooperation within the workplace may not be the same, especially when it comes time to discuss the matter at the joint health and safety committee level. Perseverance will be required. The committee is a forum for concretely addressing health and safety hazards and union members must use it to push for change.

Mapping

Mapping techniques can also be used in your workplace, both to identify the stress hazards and the health effects. Mapping is based on the idea that "a picture is worth a thousand words." It uses basic visual and participatory action research principles. By representing hazards and their effects visually, they can be more easily recognised and more clearly expressed than by written explanations.

Mapping is a participant-driven form of collecting information that recognises workers as a source of valuable information and producers of knowledge.

Three types of mapping are typically used to assess a health and safety hazard: body mapping, hazard mapping and your world mapping. Body mapping shows the physical and psychological effects of stress hazards. Hazard mapping looks at the layout of a workplace, charting where hazards exist. These three forms of mapping provide a complete picture of health and safety hazards.

TAKING ACTION

Right to Refuse

Employers have a legal responsibility to provide a safe and healthy workplace under both Canadian federal and provincial health and safety legislation. This principle is commonly known as the general duty clause. It applies to stress.

The employer and/or the joint health and safety committee must then investigate the work refusal. If the matter is not resolved, a government occupational health and safety officer must intervene to facilitate a resolution.

Traditionally, the right to refuse has been used in other areas, such as with possible exposure to toxic chemicals or cases where workers are required to work in confined spaces without proper engineering controls.

Stress is a health and safety hazard that can entitled to coffee and lunch breaks, make sure create unsafe working conditions. A work refusal you are taking these breaks. Refusing unsafe work on the grounds that stress is a hazard forces the employer and the joint health and safety committee to deal with stress.

Provisions that define breaks and the length of work days ensure that workers get a proper rest from work and that they are paid for all of the time they spend working.

The body and mind need to rest. A fifteen minute break can really help. Taking a break reminds members that they have some control over their job. Asserting control is central to eliminating workplace stress.

Worker Control

Workplaces need to foster a supportive work-place climate to help eliminate stress, for example, by not tolerating bullying, harassment and violence in any form. Workers need control for their jobs to be fulfilling. Work must be a meaningful part of our lives.

A Supervisors need to be supportive of workers, more democratic workplace is a safer and healthier workplace.

For example, by listening to workers' ideas and concerns and acknowledging workers' contributions to the workplace. Leave days should be provided to permit workers time for childcare, elder care and personal reasons. Employers should provide Employee Assistance Programs (EAPs) as a way to counter the effects of stress, keeping in mind that these programs do not replace the need for employers to prevent and eliminate workplace stressors.

Workers also need to fully utilise existing controls to combat stress. Likewise, workers must insist that stress hazards be inspected and investigated by joint health and safety committees or health and safety representatives at their workplaces. Actions such as these are good examples whereby workers can exercise their existing control to help prevent stress.

Stress Policy

A policy is a good starting point for change on a health and safety issue. The health and safety committee in your workplace should be instrumental in tabling and pushing for the adoption of a workplace stress prevention policy. A policy would start from the premise that stress is an occupational health and safety hazard, and that all steps possible should be taken to prevent the hazard.

Further specifics could be added to the policy. For example, it could have anti-bullying and anti-harassment statements that aim to get rid of workplace stress. A policy could also include a statement about the pace of work, whereby any pace of work that creates stress, and thereby poses a health and safety hazard, should be prohibited.

The exact range of a stress policy in a given workplace may vary. What should be central is the universal principle of health and safety law in this country: the employer is obligated to protect workers' health.

A good policy paves the way for further solutions and strategies, for example, collective bargaining language on stress, the role of the joint health and safety committee, and even changes to legislation. Any policy should be reviewed from time to time to assess its effectiveness. Policies can be updated and revised if necessary.

Stress Health and Safety Contract Language

Stress can be addressed through collective bargaining. Collective agreements should always aim to improve workers' health and safety. Because stress is largely caused by how work is organised, collective agreements can be used to reorganise work to eliminate stress hazards.

Any collective agreement language on stress should have prevention of the hazard at its core. A definition of workplace stress should be spelled out in the collective agreement to frame stress hazards. The concept of normal versus toxic stress could be mentioned in the definition.

Language should set some limits on workers' job descriptions to avoid toxic stress working conditions. Collective bargaining should consider provisions that aim to reduce and eliminate stress, such as:

— Set minimum staffing levels.

— Establish flextime and job sharing initiatives.

— Create more favorable shift arrangements and permit workers to swap shifts with each other to accommodate family and other responsibilities. Set limits to overtime.

— Create shorter or compressed work Jlls weeks.

— Allow for voluntary reduced hours at work to accommodate personal or family needs. While working reduced hours, workers keep their full-time status, seniority and full benefits.
— Establish sufficient rest breaks.
— Create childcare provisions and parental leaves to address work-family imbalances.
— Provide time and resources for members to receive union health and safety training on stress and other health and safety issues.

Language should include provisions for the joint health and safety committee to investigate stress hazards and to make recommendations for improvements.

Any local entering into collective bargaining should look at their stress situation and push to integrate stress language into their collective agreement. Research has shown that any benefits that come from stress management programs are merely temporary and are lost if workers return to a work environment where stressors remain unchanged. Do not negotiate for wellness programs and other such schemes as these will not prevent stress hazards.

Stress Legislation and Regulations

While Canada has no explicit stress legislation or regulations, the responsibility for providing a healthy and safe workplace still rests with employers. This responsibility is known as the general duty clause. But it does not go far enough to prevent stress hazards. Legislation is needed that explicitly covers stress as a health and safety hazard.

There are legislative examples from other parts of the world that address workplace stress. In Denmark, the Order on the Performance of Work is a regulation of the Work Environment Act.

In Sweden, the Working Environment Act says work content, technology and organisation must be: "designed in such a way that they do not expose the workers to undesirable physical and mental damage due to excessive strain that leads them to suffer sickness and accidents." The Swedish law further states that work should aim to: "involve a compensation in the form of diversity in work, satisfaction, social participation and personal development." The Swedish Work Authority has also started a program to recruit new health and safety inspectors with psychosocial and work organisation qualifications. These inspectors are being sent out to workplaces to inspect stress, workload, and other work organisation hazards.

Similar legislation could be beneficial in Canada for eliminating stress. Also, the language from the Scandinavian examples could be integrated into stress collective agreement clauses and policies in Canadian workplaces.

Of course, legislation on the books is only part of the battle. As with other health and safety hazards, enforcement of the law is fundamental to ensure workers' health and safety is protected.

References

Buss D.M. (Ed.), *The handbook of evolutionary psychology* (pp. 724–746). New York: Wiley.

Di Martino, V. & Mohtar, M. (2001). *Guidance for the Prevention of Stress and Violence at the Workplace.* Kuala Lumpur: Department of Occupational Safety and Health Malaysia.

Geary, D.C. (1998). *Male, female: The evolution of human sex differences.* Washington, DC: APA Press.

Maslach, C. (1998). Burnout. In J.M. Stellman (Ed.), *Encyclopaedia of Occupational Health and Safety* (pp. 34.64). Geneva: International Labour Office.

9

Organisational Socialisation

Work organisations offer a person far more than merely a job. Indeed, from the time individuals first enter a workplace to the time they leave their membership behind, they experience and often commit themselves to a distinct way of life complete with its own rhythms, rewards, relationships, demands, and potentials. To be sure, the differences to be found within and between organisations range from the barely discernible to the starkly dramatic.

By and large, studies of work behaviour have, to date, focused primarily upon the ahistorical or "here and now" behaviour and attitudes assumed by individual members of an organisation that are associated with various institutional, group, interactional, and situational attributes. Relatively less attention has been given to the manner in which these responses are thought to arise. In particular, the question of how it is that only certain patterns of thought and action are passed from one generation of organisational members to the next has been neglected.

Any organisational culture consists broadly of long standing rules of thumb, a somewhat special language and ideology that help edit a member's everyday experience, starred standards of relevance as to the critical aspects of the work that is being accomplished, matter-of-fact prejudices, models for social etiquette and demeanor, certain customs and rituals suggestive of how members are to relate to colleagues, subordinates, superiors, and outsiders, and a sort of residual category of some rather plain "horse sense" regarding what is appropriate and "smart" behaviour within the organisation and what is not.

Such cultural forms are so rooted in the recurrent problems and common experiences of the membership in an organisational segment that once learned they become viewed by insiders as perfectly "natural" responses to the world of work they inhabit. This is merely to say that organisational cultures arise and are maintained as a way of coping with and making sense of a given problematic environment. That organisations survive the lifetimes of their founders is then to suggest that the culture established by the original membership displays at least some stability through time. Thus, the devout believer is the Church's way of ensuring the survival of the Church; the loyal citizen Is the State's way of ensuring the survival of the State: the scientific apprentice is Physics' way of ensuring the survival of Physics; and the productive employee is the Corporation's way of ensuring the survival of the Corporation.

This is not to say, however, that the transfer of a particular work culture from generation to generation of organisational participants occurs smoothly, quickly, aid without evolutionary difficulty. New members always bring with them at least the potential for change. They may, for example, question old assumptions about how the work is to be performed, be Ignorant of some rather sacred interpersonal conventions that define authority relationships within the workplace, or fail to properly appreciate the work ideology or organisational mandate shared by the more experienced members present on the scene.

The more experienced members must therefore find ways to insure that the newcomer does not disrupt the on-going activity on the scene, embarrass or cast a disparaging light on others, or question too many of the established cultural solutions worked out previously. The manner in which this teaching/learning occurs is referred to here as the organisational socialisation process.

At heart, organisational socialisation is a jejune phrase used by social scientists to refer to the process by which one is taught and learns "the ropes" of a particular organisational role. In its most general sense, organisational socialisation is then the process by which an individual acquires the social knowledge and skills necessary to assume an organisational role. Across the roles, the process may appear in many forms ranging from a relatively quick, self-guided, trial-and-error process to a far more elaborate one requiring a lengthy preparation period of education and training followed by an equally drawn out period of official apprenticeship. At any rate, given a particular role, organisational socialisation refers minimally, though, as we shall see, not maximally, to the fashion in which an individual is taught and learns what behaviours and perspectives are customary and desirable within the work setting as well as what ones are not.

Insofar as the individual is concerned, the results of an organisational socialisation process include, for instance, a readiness to select certain events for attention over others, a stylised stance toward one's routine activities, some ideas as to how one's various behavioural responses to recurrent situations are viewed by others, and so forth. To come to know an organisational situation and act within it implies that a person has developed some commonsensical beliefs, principles, and understandings, or in shorthand notation, a perspective for interpreting one's experiences in a given sphere of the work world. Once developed, a perspective provides a person with the conventional wisdom that governs a particular context as to the typical features of everyday life.

To illustrate this highly contingent and contextual process, consider the following hypothetical, but completely piausible exchange between an experienced patrolman and a colleague in a police department. When asked about what happened to him on a given shift, the veteran officer night well respond by saying, "we didn't do any police work, just wrote a couple of movers and brought In a body, a stand-up, you know." The raw recruit could hardly know of such things for the description given clearly presumes a special kind of knowledge shared by experienced organisational members as to the typical features of their work and how such knowledge is used when going about and talking about their job.

At this point, however, it is Important to note that not all organisational socialisation can be assumed to be functional for either the individual or the organisation. Organisations are created and sustained by people often for other people and are also embedded deeply within a larger and continually changing environment:. They invent as well as provide the means by which Individual and collective needs are fulfilled. Consider, for example, the pervasive practice in many relatively stable organisations of encouraging most lower and middle managerial employees to aspire to high position with. In the organisation despite the fact that there will be very few positions open at these levels. Perhaps the discontent of the so-called "plateaued manager" can then be seen as a result of a socialisation practice that has outlived its usefulness.

Consider also that what may be adjustlve for the individual may not be adaptive for the organisation. Situations in which the careless assignment of an eager and talented newcomer to an indifferent, disgruntled, or abrasively cantankerous supervisor may represent such a case wherein the adjustive solution seised upon by the new member is to leave the organisation as soon as employment elsewhere has been secured. Socialisation practices must not therefore be taken-for-grahted or, worse, ignored on the basis that all cultural learning is fundamentally functional.

We must note also that the problems of organisational socialisation refer to any and all passages undergone by members of an organisation. From beginning to end, a person's career within an organisation represents a potential series of transitions from one position to another. These transitions may be few in number or many, they may entail upward, downward, or lateral movement, and demand relatively mild to severe adjustments on the part of the individual. Of course, the intensity, importance, and visibility of a given passage will vary across a person's career. It is probably most obvious when a person first enters the organisation — the outsider to insider passage. It is perhaps least obvious when an experienced member of an organisation undergoes a simple change of assignment, shift, or job location.

Background and Underlying Assumptions

With few exceptions, observers of organisations have failed to give systematic attention to the problem of how specific bits of culture are transmitted within an organisation. The empirical materials that do exist are scattered widely across all disciplines found in the social sciences and hence do rot share a common focus or a set of similar concepts. Even within sociology and aithropology, the disciplines most concerned with cultural matters, the published studies devoted to socialisation practices of groups, organisations, subcultures, societies, tribes, and so forth tend to be more often than not anecdotal, non-comparative, and based upon retrospective informant accounts of the process rather than the observation of the process in situ.

Our efforts are directed toward building a sound theoretical base for the study of organisational socialisation and not toward proffering any normative theory as the "effectiveness" or "ineffectiveness" of any give organisational form. Such a theory, to be analytically sound, must accomplish at least three things.

First, it must tell us where to look within an organisation to observe socialisation in its most salient and critical forms. Second, such a theory must describe in a fashion generally applicable to a large number of organisational contexts the various cultural forms organisational socialisation can take. And, third, the theory must offer some explanation as to why a particular form of a socialisation occuring at a given location within an organisation tends to result in certain kinds of individual or collective outcomes rather than others.

Some Assumptions

There are, of course, many assumptions that undergird our theory building efforts in this regard. First, and perhaps of most importance, is the well grounded assumption that individuals undergoing any organisational transition are in an anxiety producing situation. In the main, they are %ore or less motivated to reduce this anxiety by learning the functional and social requirements of their newly assumed role as quickly as possible. The sources of this anxiety are many. To wit, psychological tensions are promoted no doubt by the feelings of loneliness and isolation that are associated initially with a new location in an organisation as well as the performance anxieties a person may have when assuming new duties. Thus, stress is likely because newcomers to a Particular organisational role will initially feel a lack of identification with the various activities observed to be going on about them. Needless to say, different kinds of transitions will invoke different levels of anxiety, but any passage from the familiar to the less familiar will create some difficulties for the person moving on.

Second, organisational socialisation and the learning that is associated with it does not occur in a social vacuum strictly on the basis of the official and available versions of the new role requirements. Colleagues, superiors, subordinates, clients, and other associates support and guide the individual in learning the new role. Indeed, they help to interpret the events one experiences such that one can eventually take action in one's altered situation. Ultimately, they provide the individual with a sense of accomplishment and competence.

Third, the stability and productivity of any organisation depends in large measure upon the ways newcomers to various positions come to eventually carry out their tasks. When the passing of positions from generation to generation of incumbents is accomplished smoothly with a minimum of disruption, the continuity of the organisation's mission is maintained, the predictability of the organisation's performance is left intact. It could be said that the various socialisation processes carried out within an organisation represent the glue which holds together the various interlocking parts of an on-going social concern.

Fourth, the way in which individuals adjust to novel circumstances is remarkably similar though there is no doubt great variation in the particular content and type of adjustments achieved. In some cases, a shift into a new work situation may result in a sharply altered organisational and personal identity for an individual as often occurs when a factory worker becomes a foreman or a staff analyst becomes a line manager. In other cases, the shift may result in only minor and insignificant changes in a person's organisational and personal identity as perhaps is the case when a craftsnan is rotated to a new department or a fireman changes from working the hook-and-ladder to a rescue squad. Yet, in any of these shifts there is still likely to be at least some surprise or what Hughes horizon calls "reality shock" in store for the individual involved when he first encounters the new working context. In short, rarely, if ever, can such learning be complete until a newcomer has endured a period of initiation within the new role. As Barnard horizon noted with characteristic clarity, "there is no instant replacement, there is always a period of adjustment."

Fifth, the analysis that follows makes no so-called functional assumptions about the necessity of organisations to socialise individuals to particular kinds of roles. Indeed, we reject any implicit or explicit notions that certain organisationally relevant rules, values, or motivations must be internalised by people as "blueprints for behaviour" if they are to participate and contribute to the organisation's continued survival. While, there are no doubt reasons why certain socialisation tactics are used more frequently by one organisation rather than another, these reasons are to be located at the human level of analysis, not at the structural or functional levels. From this perspective, we are very much committed to a symbolic interactionist view of social life, one that suggests that individuals, not organisations, create and sustain beliefs about what is and is not functional.

Sixth, and finally, we assume here that a theory of organisational socialisation must not allow itself to become too preoccupied with individual characteristics specific organisations or particular occupational roles. To be of value to researchers and laymen alike, the theory must transcend the particular and peculiar, and aim for the general and typical. At least at this stage in the construction of a theory, there are, as we will show, some rather recognisable and pervasive socialisation processes used across virtually all organisational settings and all kinds of individuals that can be understood far more quickly and directly if we do not bog ourselves down In the examination of every dimension that conceivably could influence the outcome of a given process. In other words, the theory we sketch out below does not seek to specify its own applications or uniqueness.

Organisational Setting

Perhaps the best way to view an organisation follows the anthropological line suggesting that any group of people who interact regularly over an extended period of time will develop a sort of unexplicated or tacit mandate concerning what is correct and proper for a member of the group to undertake as well as what is the correct and proper way to go about such an undertaking. At a high level of abstraction, then, members of on-going business organisations, for example, orient their efforts toward "making money" in socially prescribed ways just as members of governmental agencies orient their efforts toward "doing public service" in socially prescribed ways. More concretely, however, organisations are made up of people each following ends that are to some degree unique. Over time, these negotiations result in an emerging set of organisationally defined roles for people to fill. These roles may or may not be formalised and fully sanctioned throughout the organisation yet they nonetheless appear to have some rather stable properties associated with them which tend to be passed on from role taker to role taker. Of course, these organisationaly defined roles hardly coerce each role taker to perform in identical ways. Certainly, whenever a novel problem arises, people come together acting within their roles to confront and make sense of the shared event. Such events, if serious enough, give rise to altered definitions of both the organisational role and the organisational situation in which the role is carried out.

The problem we face here concerns the manner in which these versions of what people are to do — organisationally defined roles — are passed on and interpreted from one role occupant to the next. To do so, however, requires a model of the organisation such that members can be distinguished from one another and from outsiders on the basis of as few organisational variables as possible. Furthermore, we need a model that is flexible enough to allow for as much descriptive validity as possible across a wide variety of organisational contexts.

Schein has developed a model of the organisation that provides a quite useful description of an organisationally defined role in terms of three dimensions that are discernable empirically. The first dimension is functional one and refers to the various tasks performed by members of an organisation. Thus, most organisations have departmental structures which for enterprises located in to business sector of the economy might include the functions of marketing, finance, production, administrative staff, personnel, research and development, and so forth. Visually, we can map the functional domains of an organisation along departmental and subdepartmental or program lines as if each function and srab-function occupied a part of a circle or pie-shaped figure. Each function then covers a particular portion of the circumference of the circle depending upon its proportionate size within the organisation.

Bach slice in the figurative representation is a functional division with relatively distinct boundaries such thatt most persons in the organisation could easily locate themselves and others within a slice of the circle. Clearly, no two organisations would be precisely the same because even if the department and subdepartment structures were identical, the numbers of people contained within each slice would no doubt differ.

The second dimension Identified by Schein concern the hierarchical distribution of rank within an organisation. This is essentially a matter of who, on paper, is responsible for the actions of whom.

According to the model, very decentralised organisations will have, for example, relatively few hierarchical distinctions whereas very centralised organisations will have many. Mapping this dimension on paper, it would typically take a triangular shape wherein the highest ranks are held by relatively few people located at the apex.

The XYS Widget Company is perhaps the most typical in that it fits textbook models of a management structure wherein increasing rank is assumed by decreasing numbers of people in a relatively smooth way. Metropolitan Police Department is representative of a large number of service bureaucracies. These agencies have been tagged "street level" organisations because, in part, most of their membership occupies positions that carry low rank. To wit, over 75 percent of the employees in most police organisations work as patrolmen or investigators, the lowest ranked positions in these organisations. Sipper Sales, Inc. illustrates an organisation with a very steep authority structure within which each rank supervises relatively few people but there are many ranks. The Sero Research Institute displays what a relatively flat hierarchical structure looks like in this schema Here there are few ranks for members to seek to ascend. Finally, the Stuffed Mattress Corporation is included here to demonstrate something of the range of possiblities available to describe the hierarchical spread which potentially can characterise an organisation.

The third dimension in Schein's model is the most difficult to conceptualise and concerns the social fabric or interpersonal domain of organisational life. This is fundamentally an interactional dimension and refers to a persons inclusion within the organisation. It can be depicted as if it were a radial dimension extending from the membership edge of a slice of organisational members in toward the middle of the functional circle. One moves toward the "centre of things" or away toward the "periphery." When examining this dimension, the question must be asked how important to others on the immediate scene is a given member's role in the workings of a particular group, department, or organisation? Thus, this radial dimension must involve the social rules, norms, and values through which a person's worthiness to a group is judged by members of that group. It concerns in part, then, the shared notions of what the "realwork" of any organisational segment is at any given time.

Newcomers to most hierarchical levels and functional areas in virtually all organisations inevitably remain "on the edge" of organisational affairs for some time after entrance for a host of reasons. They may not yet be deemed trustworthy by other members on the seen. Or, quite typically, newcomers must first be tested either informally or formally as to their abilities, motives, and values before being granted inclusionary rights which then permit them:

1) to share organisational secrets,

2) to separate the presentational rhetoric used on outsiders to speak of what goes on in the setting from the operational rhetoric used by insiders to communicate with one another as to the matters-at-hand, and/or

3) to understand the unofficial yet recognised norms associated with the actual work going on and the moral conduct expected of people in the particular organisational segment.

In other words, movement along the inclusionary dimension is analogous to the entrance of a stranger to any group. If things go well, the stranger is granted more say in the group's activities and is given more opportunity to display his or her particular skills thus becoming in the process more central and perhaps valuable to the group as a whole. In short, to cross inclusionary boundaries means that one becomes an insider with all the rights and privileges that go with such a position. In certain educational Institutions, the granting of university tenure represents the formal recognition of crossing a major inclusionary boundary, as well as the more obvious hierarchical passage.

When the three dimensions — functional, hierarchical, and inclusionary — are combined, the model of the organisation becomes analytically most useful and interesting. From a Weberian, ideal-type perspective, organisations are conical in shape and contain within them three generic types of boundaries across which a member may pass. And, as Schein suggests, these boundaries will differ within and between organisations as to both their number and permeability. Relatively tall organisations may have, for example, many hierarchical boundaries yet relatively few functional and inclusionary ones. By implication, members moving up or down in such organisations must orient themselves more to rank and level distinctions among the membership than to the distinctions which result from either functional specialisation or social status within a given rank. On the other hand, flat organisations such as some consulting firms have few hierarchical boundaries but many functional and inclusionary ones. Indeed, in such firms, turnover is high and few members are allowed to pass across the relatively stringent radial dimensions to become central and permanent fixtures within the organisation. Prestigious universities represent another good illustration wherein functional boundaries are exceedingly difficult to rotate through and inclusionary boundaries are guarded by the most rigorous of tenuring policies.

Organisations also differ In the sorts of filtering processes they use to screen, select, and process those members who pass across particular boundaries. Hierarchical boundaries crossed by persons moving upward are associated usually with filtering processes carrying notions of merit, potential, and judged past performance, although age and length of service are often utilised as surrogate measures of "readiness" to move upward in an organisation. Functional boundaries usually filter people on the basis of their demonstrated skill or assumed aptitude to handle a particular task. Finally, inclusionary filters, in the main, represent evaluations made by others on the scene as to another "fitness" for membership. Of course, such evaluations may be formal, informal, or both. Consider the new patrolman in a large urban police department who must not only serve out a period of official probation successfully but also must pass a number of unofficial colleague-initiated tests on the street before others in the department will view him as a desirable member of the patrol division within the organisation.

Given this model, some key postulates about the socialisation process in organisations can be stated.

First, socialisation/ although continuous throughout one's career within an organisation, is no doubt more intense and problematic for a member just before and just after a particular boundary passage. That is, an individual's anxiety and hence vulnerability to organisational influence are likely to be highest during the anticipatory and initiation phases of an organisational boundary passage.

Similarly, the more boundaries that are crossed by a person at any one time, the more profound the experience is likely to be for the person. This is one reason why the outsider-to-insider passage in which an individual crosses over all three organisational boundaries at once is so often marked by dramatic changes in a person, changes of a sort that are rarely matched again during other internal passages of the individual's career.

Second, a person is likely to have the most impact upon others in the organisation, what Porter, Lawler, and Hackman horizon call the "individualisation" process and what Schein horizon refers to as the "innovation" process, at points furthest from any boundary crossing.

Third, because of the conical shape typically displayed by organisations, socialisation along the inclusionary dimension is likely to be more critical to lower placed members than higher placed members since, according to the model, to move up in the organisation indicates that some, perhaps considerable movement has already occurred invard. Consider, for example those business concerns whose top executives invariably come from only certain functional areas of the organisation. Similarly, organisations may also be tipped radically to the side. In such cases, certain inclusionary prerequisites for career movements and their associated boundary passages have been more or less altered because "insiders" at one level are "outsiders" at another. Nor are "insiders" in a favorable position to move upward in the organisation as might be the case in more symmetrically shaped firms where certain key values are shared by all "insiders" regardless of level. Yet, it is probably also true that during such a climb the climber has little effect upon any of the various groups in which he or she may have claimed membership since the climber will never have developed a persuasive or influential position within these organisational segments.

We have now reached the stage where it makes sense to return to the individual level of analysis for a time and consider the ways in which people can respond to an organisational socialisation process. And, after considering this problem briefly, we can then proceed to the central matters of our concern, the examination of various processes through which organisationally defined roles are passed on from generation to generation of organisational members.

Knowledge, Strategy, and Mission

Any organisationally defined role includes what Hughes horizon called a "bundle of tasks". Whether one is~ a lathe operator, dentist, beauty operator, or computer programer, each role includes many specific actions and tasks to be performed ranging from perhaps sweeping the floor to mediating disputes between colleagues, or, from filling in for an absent coworker to utilising one's own somewhat special and unique skills in the performance of a given task. In general, then, a role is merely the set of often diverse behaviours that are more or less expected of persons who occupy a certain defined position within a particular social system, in this case, an organisation. If not, however, it usually follows that certain remedial actions are taken or punishments meted out.

All roles which are created, sustained, and transmitted by people include both content characteristics and process characteristics. The content of a particular role can be depicted both in terms of a general, almost ideological mandate that goes with it and in terms of the practical set of mandate-fulfilling actions that are supposed to be performed by the role occupant. Thus, doctors are thought to "heal the sick" by prescribing available "cures" to be found somewhere within the vast catalogue of "medical" knowledge." Similarly, the process associated with the performance of a role also has associated with it general strategies and specific practices. The doctor "does diagnosis" by talcing a patient's blood pressure, eliciting a history, reading an X-ray, and so forth.

Putting these conceptual matters together, organisationally defined roles can be seen to possess, first, a content or knowledge base which, If accepted by the role occupant, indicates the range of existing solutions to the given problems encountered regularly on the job. Engineers know, for instance, the heat limits to which certain metals can be exposed before the molecules of the metals rearrange themselves. Second, an organisationally defined role includes a strategic base which suggests the groundrules for the chosing of particular solutions. Hence, engineers may be out to "cut costs" or "beat the competition" in some organisations when designing a particular product or piece of machinery. Third, organisationally defined roles are invested historically with something of an explicit and implicit mission, purpose, or mandate which is, in part, traceable to the knowledge and strategy bases of the role, but, also is grounded in the total organisational mission and in the relationships that a particular role has with other roles within and outside the organisation. While the professionalisation of a particular occupational role can be viewed as an attempt to reduce such dependencies through the claim made by role practitioners to have an autonomous and special knowledge base, such professionalisation in an organisational society such organisationally defined roles serve to legitimate, justify, and define the ends pursued by role occupants and, thus, support to some degree the various strategies and norms followed by those presently performing the role.

These three features of an organisationally defined role — knowledge base, strategy, and mission — and the norms that surround them are of course highly intertwined. A change in the knowledge base of a given role may alter the means and end followed by practitioners. Indeed, the recognised failure to achieve a given end may provoke the development of new knowledge.

Strategic failures are not unknown either and may lead to the disenchantment and change in the mission and knowledge bases of a particular role.

Responses to Socialisation

Custodianship, Content Innovation, and Role Innovation

Perhaps the easiest or most expedient response of a newcomer to a given role is to assume a custodial or caretaker stance toward the knowledge, strategies, and missions associated with the role. Taking such a stance, the newcomer does not question but accepts the status quo. First and foremost among them is the plain fact that the inherited past assumed by the newcomer may have much to recommend it in terms of functional achievement. If the enterprise has been successful, why "rock the boat"?

One simply learns the substantive requirements of the job and the customary strategies that have been developed to meet these requirements and the successful accomplishment of the mission is assured.

On the other hand, as a newcomer one may feel for a variety of reasons somewhat impatient with or uneasy about the knowledge base of a particular organisational role that is transmitted and, hence, be unwilling to limit oneself to the use of such knowledge in the performance of the role. A newly promoted marketing manager may, for instance, take issue with the quality of some of the regional reports used by his or her predecessor to inform Ms decision making, the new manager may then aggresively seek out other information on which to base his decisions. Similarly, tactical alternatives as to the means to certain ends may be sought out by individuals after assuming a new role. The new marketing manager may decide to involve more salesmen and engineers in group meetings devoted to developing new product lines instead of relying only on his or her own marketing people.

Schein refers to this response as "content innovation." It is marked by the development of substantive improvements or changes in the knowledge base or strategic practices of a particular role. In such cases, traditional ends and norms of practice are accepted by the newcomer, but the person is troubled by the existing strategies or teehnologies-in-use for the achievement of these ends and perhaps is troubled too by the degree to which the traditional norms are circumvented in practice.

Pushing the analysis one more step, an individual may seek to redefine the entire role by attacking and attempting to change the mission associated traditionally with that role. This response is characterised by a complete rejection of most of the norms governing the conduct and performance of a particular role. The "Rebel" or "Guerrilla" or "Insurgent" are popular tags we attach to and associate with such responses. Take, for example, Ralph Nader's attempts within certain communities of lawyers who work for the federal government to create and sustain an organisationally defined role of consumer advocate, industrial safety proponent, or even whistle-blower. Also note the recent questioning raised by health care officials as to the appropriate aims of medical practice. Schein has called this response "role innovation" in that a genuine attempt is made by a role holder to redefine the ends which the role functions.

Thus, there are two poles toward which a newcomers response to an organisationally defined role can gravitate. At one extreme is the caretaking response, marked by an acceptance of the role as presented and traditionally practiced by role occupants. We will label this response and the various forms it can take as "custodial". At the other extreme, we can group responses of an "innovative" nature. Lerhaps most extreme are those responses which display a rejection and redefinition of the major premises concerning missions and strategies followed by the majority of the role occupants to both practice and justify their present role — what we label here ''role innovation". Of course, such new knowledge, if discovered, %ay lead only to a further rationalisation of the present practices and goals, but, nevertheless, the search Itself, to differing degrees, represents something of an innovative response. For our purposes then, those individuals who after assuming a given role, seek actively to alter its knowledge base, strategic practices, or historically established ends display a generic response type we will label "innovative" and which can be further broken down into role innovation and content innovation.

The central but still nagging question-remains, of course, as to the reasons that provoke one or the other response types. Certainly, individuals vary in their backgrounds, value systems, and predispostlons to calmly accept things as they are or to vigorously strive to alter them. It is true too that changes in the larger environment within which organisationally defined roles are played out may force certain changes upon role occupants despite perhaps vehement resistance or whatever particular backgrounds, values, or predispositions define those who presently perform a given role. The causal mechanism we seek to examine here is the organisational socialisation process itself. Therefore, the arguement to follow suggests that there are particular forms of socialisation that can enhance or retard the likelihood of an innovative or custodial response to an organisationally defined role no matter what the attributes of the people being processed or how the particular environment is characterised within which the process occurs.

TACTICS OF IORGANISATIONAL SOCIALISATION

The phrase, "tactics of organisational socialisation" refers to the ways in which the experiences of an individual in transition from one role to another are structured for him by others in the organisation. These tactics may be selected consciously by the management of an organisation such as the requirement that all newcomers attend a formal training session or orientation program of some kind before assuming the duties of a particular role. From the perspective of those learning the role, the selection of teaching methods is often made by persons not of their own situation but rather by those long gone. Yet, these choices may still bind contemporary members of the organisation. Or, teaching methods may arise simply from certain latent and unexamined premises or assumptions underlying present practices.

Individual in transition and which may make innovative responses from that individual more likely than custodial. It is possible therefore to denote the various tactics used by organisations and then to explore the differential results of their use upon the people to whom they are directed.

That is, we are interested in describing various forms and results of socialisation as they occur when persons move across hierarchical, functional, and inclusionary boundaries. The main focus is consequently upon the external or structural properties peculiar to a specified tactic. The tactics are essentially process variables akin to, but more specific than such general transitional processes as education, training, apprenticeship, or sponsorship. Theoretically, at least, they can be used in virtually any setting in which individual careers are played out be they business careers, school careers, political careers, service careers, blue, white, or pink collar careers, civil service careers, and so on. The analysis follows, then, the most fundamental premise that people respond to particular organisationally defined roles differently not only because people and organisations differ, but also because socialisation processes differ.

Each tactic we discuss below operates in a way that somewhat uniquely organises the learning experiences of a newcomer to a particular role. Although much of the evidence presented here on the effects of a given strategy comes from studies conducted on the outsider-to-insider passage wherein a person first becomes a member of the organisation, the analysis seems to go beyond these transitions by examining the effects of each tactic across the three organisational boundaries separately, reinforcing, at the same time, the proposition that socialisation occurs periodically throughout the organisational careers of individuals.

The various tactics we will describe are not mutually exclusive. Indeed, they are usually combined in sundry and sometimes inventive ways. The effects of the tactics upon people are consequently cumulative. Additionally, each tactic is discussed along with its counterpart or opposing tactic. In other words, each can be thought of as existing on a continuum where there is a considerable range between the two poles.

The term tactic"is used here to describe each of the listed processes because the degree to which any one tactic is used by an organisation is not in any sense a "natural" or prerequisite condition necessary for socialisation to occur. In other words, socialisation itself always takes place at boundary transitions by some means or other. Paid, whether the tactics used are selected by design or accident, they are at least theoretically subject to rapid and complete change at the direction of the management of an organisation.

Van Maanen horizon has identified at least six major tactical dimensions which characterise the structural side of organisational socialisation. These dimensions or processes were deduced logically from empirical observations and from accounts found in the social science literature. We do not assert here that this list is exhaustive or that the processes are presented in any order of relevance to a particular organisation or occupation. We do assert however and attempt to demonstrate that these tactics are quite common to a given boundary passage and of substantial consequence to people in the organisation in that they partially determine the degree to which the response of the newcomer will be custodial or innovative.

Lastly, we should note that there is seemingly no logical or conclusive end to a list of organisational socialisation tactics. The list may well be infinite for these are essentially cultural forms that are continually subject to invention and modification as well as stabilisation and continuity. Our reasons for choosing these particular tactics are simply the visible presence of a tactic across what appears to be a wide variety of organisations as veil as the seeming importance and power of that tactic on persons who are subjected to it.

The six dimensions we will analyse are:

1) Collective vs. individual socialisation processes
2) Formal vs. informal socialisation processes
3) Sequential vs. random steps in the socialisation process
4) Fixed vs. variable socialisation processes
5) Serial vs. distructive socialisation processes
6) Investiture vs. divestiture socialisation processes

Collective vs. Individual Socialisation Processes

Collective socialisation refers to the tactic of taking a group of recruits who are facing a given boundary passage and putting them through a common set of experiences together.

At the other extreme, socialisation in the individual mode refers to the tactic of processing recruits singly and in isolation from one another through a more or less unique set of experiences. Apprenticeship programs, specific intern or trainee assignments, and plain "on-the-job training" wherein a recruit is expected to learn a given organisationally defined role on his or her own accord are typical examples. In the unit or made-to-order case, recruits are processed individually through a rather different series of events with the results being relatively variable.

As Becker horizon and others have argued quite persuasively, when Individuals experience a socialisation program collectively, the thoughts, feelings, and actions of those in the recruit group almost always reflect an "in the same boat" consciousness. Individual changes in perspective are therefore built upon an understanding of the problems faced by all group members.

Collective socialisation processes often promote and intensify the demands of the socialisation agents% Indeed, army recruits socialise each other in ways the army could never do, or, for that matter, would not officially be permitted to do. Similarly, graduate students are often said to learn more from one another than from the faculty. And, while the socialisation agents may have the power to define the nature of the collective problem, the recruits often have more resources available to them to define the solution — time, experience, motivation, expertise and patience. In many cases, collective tactics result in formation of an almost separate subworld within the organisation comprised solely of recruits,.complete with its own argot, areas of discourse, and unique understandings. A cultural perspective is developed that can be brought to bear upon common problems faced by the group. Sharing similar difficulties and working out collective solutions clearly dramatised to the recruits the worth and usefulness of colleagual relationships.

Individual strategies also induce personal change. But the views adopted by people processed individually are likely to be far less homogeneous than the views of those processed collectively. In psychoanalytic training, for example, the vocabulary of motives a recruit-patient develops to interpret his or her situation is quite personal and specific compared to the vocabulary that develops in group therapy.

Apprenticeship modes of work socialisation are sometimes quite similar to the therapist-patient relationship. If the responsibility for transforming an individual to a given status within the organisation is delegated to only one person, an intense, value-oriented process is most likely to follow. This practice is common whenever a role incumbent is viewed by others in the organisation as being the only member capable of shaping the recruit. Since the responsibility is given to only one organisational member, the person so designated often becomes a role model whose thoughts and actions the recruit emulates. Police departments, craft-like trades, and architectural firms all make extensive use of the individual socialisation strategy. Outcomes in these one-on-one efforts are dependent primarily upon the affective relationships which may or may not develop between the apprentice and master.

However, when there are few affective bonds, the socialisation process may break down and the hoped for transition will not take place.

From this standpoint, individual socialisation processes are most likely to be associated with complex roles. Further, such modes are most frequently followed when there are relatively few incumbents compared to many aspirants for a given role and when a collective identity among recruits is viewed as less important than the recruit's learning of the operational specifics of the given role.

Formal vs. Informal Socialisation Processes

Formal socialisation refers to those processes in which a newcomer is more or less segregated from regular organisational members while being put through a set of experiences tailored explicitly for the, newcomer. Formal processes, then, leave no doubt as to the recruit's "special" role in the scheme of things organisational. These processes are illustrated by such socialisation programs as police academies, professional schools, various sorts of internships, and apprenticeships in which the activities that are to be engaged in by the apprentice are prescribed officially and clearly.

Informal socialisation processes, in contrast, do not distinguish the newcomers role specifically nor is there an effort made in such programs to rigidly differentiate the recruit from other more experienced organisational members.

This dimension is related closely to the collective-individual dimension but it is, in principle, different. While most collective socialisation processes are also formal ones, there are some which are informal. To wit, there are those situations where a cohort of new employees is brought into an organisation together, where meetings are held periodically to assess how the group is collectively getting along, but, where the work assignments of each member of the cohort are to different departments within which each member of the cohart is trained through informal means. Would be partners in law firms are often subject to such socialisation tactics whereby they must first handle the "dirty work" of the firm for some period. Certainly this sort of "pledge class of one" is not that uncommon in many occupational spheres.

Formal socialisation processes are typically found in organisations where specific preparation for new status is involved and where it is deemed important that a newcomer learn the "correct" attitudes, values, and protocol associated with the new role. To put the matter bluntly, the more formal the process, the more concern there is likely to be shown for the recruit's absorption of the appropriate demeanor and stance associated with the target role — that one begins to think and feel like a United States Marine, an I.B.M. executive, or a Catholic priest.

The greater the separation of the recruit from the day-to-day reality of the work setting, the less the newcomer will be able to carry over and generalise any abilities or skills learned in the socialisation setting. Formal processes concentrate therefore more upon attitude than act. Such results may be implicit or unintended however. Paradoxically, these newcomers are also expressing in their attitude precisely those components of the valued subcultural ethos that characterises their particular occupation — autonomy, pragmatism, and the concern for personal style.

It is important to note coo chat formal periods of socialisation not only serve to prepare recruits to assume particular statuses in an organisational world, they also serve to provide an intensive period in which others in the organisation can rather closely judge the newcomer's commitment and deference to the critical values of the occupation. Recruits in police academies are, for example, assessed quite thoroughly by staff members as to their loyalty to not only the organisation, but to their fellow recruits as well. And, those who do not adhere to particular norms thought crucial to the trade are ushered as unceremoniously out of police departments as they were ushered ceremoniously in. It is true of course that merely passing through a rigorous formal process serves also as a test the recruit's willingness to assume the new role. Often, simply the sacrifice and hard work it takes a recruit to complete a very long formal process serves to effectively fuse the newcomer to the prepared-for role.

Learning through experience in the informal socialisation mode is an entirely different matter. First, such tactics place recruits in the position where they must select their own socialisation agents. The value of this mode to the newcomer is then determined largely by the relevant knowledge possessed by an agent and, of course, the agent's ability to transfer such knowledge. The freedom of choice afforded recruits in the more informal processes has therefore a price: they must force others in the setting to teach them. Second, mistakes or errors made by recruits in an informal socialisation process must be regarded as more costly and serious than mistakes occuring in formal processes. Because real work is interfered with, a recruit who makes a mistake may create considerable trouble for both himself and others. The forgetful novice beautician who provokes a customer by dyeing her hair the wrong color may be forced to look elsewhere for an organisation in which to complete the mandatory licensing requirement of the trade. Experienced organisational members know full well that "mistakes happen" but a recruit is under a special pressure to perform well during an informal initiation period — or to at least ask before acting.

Sequential vs. Random Steps in the Socialisation Process

The degree of formality and the degree to which the process of socialisation is collective are, as indicated, associated with major boundary passages, with basic orientation activities, and, most often, with the initial entry of a recruit into the organisation. However, for some roles in an organisation, the socialisation process may cover a broad spectrum of assignments and experiences taking sometimes many years of preparation. Similarly, a person being groomed for a general manager position may have to rotate through several staff positions as a junior analyst, through various functional divisions in order to learn the "areas of the business," and through various supervisory levels to build up experiences and a so-called "good track record" which would then warrant the ultimate "goal job".

Sequential socialisation refers to the degree to which the organisation or occupation specifies a given sequence of discrete and identifiable steps leading to the target role. Random socialisation occurs when the sequence of steps leading to the target role is unknown, ambiguous, or continually changing. In the case of the general manager however, we have a sequential process only with respect to supervisory rank levels, but the sequence of rotating through functional positions and divisions is often unspecified and, in some organisations, left more or less to "random" events.

When examining sequential strategies, it is crucial to note the degree to which each stage builds or expands upon the preceding stage. For example, the courses in most technical training programs are arragned in what is thought to be a simple-to-complex progression. On the other hand, some sequential processes seem to follow no internal logic. Management education is, for instance, quite often disjointed, with the curriculum jumping from topic to topic with little integration across stages. If, however, the flow of topics or courses is harmonious and connected functionally or logically in some fashion, what may seem like minor alterations required of an individual at each sequential stage will accumulate so that at the end, persons will "discover" themselves to be considerably different than when they began. One sees this effect most clearly in the acquisition of complex skill or in the formation of a complete "professional" perspective or in the value systems built up after many years of graduate study.

Relatedly, if several agents handle various portions of a sequential process, the degree to which the aims of the agents are common is very important. Recruits quickly spot such conflicts when they exist and sometimes exploit them, playing agents off against one another. Such incongruities often lead to a more relaxed situation for the recruits, one in which they enjoy watching their instructors pay more attention to each other than they pay to the training program.

We should note that many of these concerns apply to random processes as well. In both random and sequential arrangements, agents may be unknown to one another, they may be quite far apart spatially, and may have thoroughly different images of their respective tasks. Both Merton horizon and Glaser horizon have remarked upon the difficulty many scientists apparently have when moving from a university to an industrial setting to practice their trade. The pattern is seemingly quite disconcerting for many scientists when they discover that their academic training emphasised a far different set of skills, interests, and values that is required in the corporate environment. As Avery horizon observed, to become a "good" industrial scientist, the individual has to learn the painful lesson that to be able to sell an idea Is at least as important as having one in the first place. Such a process, sometimes sequential but typically random, evocatively suggests that the person may well learn to be only whatever the immediate situation demands.

In a sequential process, there is likely to be a strong bias in the presentation by each agent to make the next stage appear benign. Thus, a recruit is told that if he will just "buckle down and apply himself" tfkUe in Stage A, Stages B, C, D, and E will be easy. Agents usually mask, unwittingly or wittingly, the true nature of the stage to follow, for, if recruits feel that the future is bright, rewarding, and assured, they will be most cooperative at the stage they are in, not wishing to risk the future they think awaits them. To wit, note the tactics of high school mathematics teachers who tell their students that if they will just work hard in algebra, geometry will be a "cinch."

Given these sensitising definitions and the qualifications that apply to this socialisation tactic, some theoretical propositions can now be stated. Propositions

Sequential socialisation is most likely to be associated with hierarchical boundaries.

Hierarchies are typically organised from the outset on the assumption that higher level positions cannot be fulfilled adequately until lower level ones have first been fulfilled. Such an assumption is not built into functional or inclusion boundaries where a person can demonstrate a readiness for passage at any given time. At least in part, hierarchies preserve sequential socialisation processes in order to maintain the image that the hierarchy itself is a valid base for the distribution of authority. Of course, in some executive promotions, skipping is accomplished for all practical purposes through the extremely rapid advancement of someone viewed as unusually talented, "fast tracked," fortuitously connected, just plain lucky, or all of these attributions together.

To pass inclusion boundaries may take a long time while one is proving oneself to be trustworthy to many different people, but the process typically does not specify a sequence in which such a test can or must be passed. In the case of functional boundaries, there may be many specific steps associated with the education or training activities involved in preparing to cross the boundary, but, sometimes at least, one may be given a job on the basis of education received at a much earlier time or on the basis of certain experiences which are seen as "equivalent" to education or training.

Sequential socialisation is more likely to produce custodial orientations among recruits than innovative orientations because the recruits remain "locked in," as it were, to the conforming demands of others in the organisation for a long period of time before the target role is achieved. And, the clearer the role, the more likely it is that the training for that role will produce a custodial response.

On the other hand, recruits who encounter various socialisation experiences in a random fashion may find themselves exposed to a wide and diverse variety of views and perceptions of the target role which would make it more likely than is true of sequential socialisation to lead to innovative orientations. It would seam therefore that a company who wishes to groom innovative general managers would do well to avoid sequential processes and encourage more ac[hoc decision making procedures in the organisation concerning managerial job moves and training experiences.

P. Fixed vs. Variable Socialisation Processes Definition

This dimension refers to the degree to which the steps involved in a socialisation process have a timetable associated with them that is both adhered to by the organisation and communicated to the recruit. Fixed socialisation processes provide a recruit with the precise knowledge of the time it will take to complete a given passage. Thus, while organisations may specify various career paths having different timetables, all of these paths may be more or less fixed in terms of the degree to which the recruit must follow the determined timetable. Similarly, others said to be on "slow" or "regular" tracks may be forewarned not to expect an assignment shift for at least four or five years. Consider also that promotional policies in most universities explicitly specify the number of years a person can be appointed to a given rank. The process can sometimes be speeded up but rarely can it be slowed down.

Variable socialisation processes give a recruit few clues as to when to expect a given boundary passage. Thus, both the prisoner of war who is told by his captors that he will be released only when he has "learned the truth" and the patient in a psychiatric hospital who cannot return home until he is again judged "normal" are in pure versions of the variable process.

Futhermore, what may be true for one person is not true for another in variable socialisation processes. Such a situation requires a recruit to search out clues as to the future. To wit, apprenticeship programs often specify only the minimum number of years a person must remain in the apprentice role and leave open the time a person can be expected to be advanced into the journeyman classification. Rumors and innuendos about who is going where and when they are going characterise situations marked by the presence of the variable strategy of socialisation. Indeed, the would be general manager often pushes quite hard to discover the signs of a coming promotion. The individual listens closely to stories concerning the time it takes one to advance in the organisation, observes as carefully as possible the experiences of others, and, in general, develops an age consciousness delineating the range of appropriate ages for given positions.

Relatedly, Roth horizon suggests that a special category of "chronic sidetrack" may be created for certain types of role failures. Thus, in the fixed socialisation processes of public schools, the retarded are shunted off to distinct classes where the notion of progress does not exist. Similarly, in some police agencies, recruits unable to meet certain agent demands, particularly during that portion of the socialisation process which is fixed and takes recruits typically through the academy to the patrol division, are provided long-term assignments as city jailors or traffic controllers, not as patrolmen. Such assignments serve as a signal to the recruit and others in the organisation that the individual has left the normal career path. To the extent that such organisational "Siberias" exist and can be identified with certainty by those in the setting, chronic sidetracking from which there is rarely a return is a distinct possibility in fixed socialisation processes. Indeed, many people who are working in the middle levels of management are often unable to judge just where they are, where they are going, or how they are doing. Consequently, variable processes are likely to create much anxiety and perhaps frustration for individuals who are unable to construct reasonably valid timetables to inform them of the appropriateness of their movement (or lack of movement) in the organisation.

It also should be noted that variable processes are a very powerful antidote to the formation of group solidarity among potential recruits to certain organisationally defined roles. The movement of people at different rates and according to different patterns makes it virtually impossible for a cohort group to remain cohesive and loyal to one another. Indeed, in highly competitive situations, recruits being processed in a variable mode tend to differentiate themselves, both socially and psychologically, from each other. Therefore, if, from the organisation's point of view, peer group solidarity in a recruit pool is desireable, care should be taken to use only fixed timetables in the socialisation processes.

Variable socialisation processes keep a recruit maximally off balance and at the mercy of socialisation agents. In fixed processes, such as a four-year medical school program, a three-month boot-camp, a one year apprenticeship, a set two-year tour of duty in another geographical district of a business firm, persons can usually gear themselves into the situation better than in the variable case and therefore can plan innovative activities to fit the timetable. This is particularly the case near the end of a given stage since others in the organisation typically also know that the innovator is now in a "lame duck" period.

Serial vs. Disjunctive Socialisation Processes Definition

A serial socialisation process is one in which experienced members of the organisation groom newcomers who are about to assume similar kinds of positions in the organisation. Serial modes create something analogous to Mead's horizon notion of a post-figurative culture. Just as children in stable societies are able to gain a sure sense of the future that awaits then by seeing in their parents and grandparents an image of themselves grown older, employees In organisations can gain a surer sense of the future by seeing in their more experienced elders an image of themselves further along in the organisation. A danger exists of course that this image will be neither flattering nor desireable from the perspective of the recruits and many newcomers may leave the organisation rather than face what appears to be an agonising future. In industrial settings where worker morale is low and turnover is high, a serial pattern of initiating newcomers into the organisation would maintain and perhaps amplify an already poor situation.

When newcomers are not following the footsteps of immediate or recent predecessors, and when no role models are available to recruits to inform them as to how they are to proceed in the new role, the socialisation process is a disjunctive one. Take, for instance, the case of a black firefighter entering a previously all white engine company or a woman entering managerial ranks in a firm that had previously been occupied only by males. In these cases, there are few, if any, persons on the scene who have shared the unique problems faced by the recruit. Certainly such situations make things extremely difficult and anxiety provoking for the newcomer. In most versions of this saga, a young man is deliberately sent away from his homeland and "suffers" through a series of trials and tribulations in order to discover new ways of thinking about and doing things.

The analytic distinction between serial and disjunctive socialisation processes is sometimes brought into sharp focus when an organisation undertakes a "house cleaning" whereby old members are swept out the back door and new members brought in the front door to replace them. In extreme cases, an entire organisation can be thrown into a disjuctive mode of socialisation with the result that the organisation will no longer resemble its former self. It is also true that occasionally the person who is presumably being socialised by another organisational member has more experience and knowledge than the one doing the socialising. To wit, in colleges where faculty members are constantly entering and exiting, long term students exert much control over the institution.

Sometimes, what appears to be a serial process is actually disjunctive. In many work organisations, it is the case that if someone is exceptionally good and is promoted to project leader by age 25, that same person must be exceptionally mediocre to be in that same position at age 50 or 55. Because of such circumstances, the age-graded stereotype of the youthful, naive, and passive junior member of the firm being coached wisely by a mature, informed, and active mentor is frequently false. Roth horizon labels this problem "gapping" and it appears to be a serious one associated with serial strategies. Gapping refers to the historical, social, or ideological distance between recruits and agents. And, when the past experiences, reference groups, or values of the agents are quite removed from those of the recruits, good intentions aside, the serial recess may become a disjunctive one.

In summary, it is generally true that recruits representing the first class will set the tone for the classes to follow. It is not suggested that those who follow are paginated seriatim, but simply that for those to come. As long as there are others available in the socialisation setting whom the newcomers consider to be "like them", these others will act as guides, passing on consensual solutions to the typical problems faced by a recruit.

Ordinarily, the degree to which the recruit experiences the socialisation process as an ordeal indicates the degree to which divestiture processes are operating. Goffman's horizon "ɩotal institutions" are commonly thought typical in this regard in the deliberate "mortifications to self" which entry into them entails. But, even in total instutitions, socialisation processes will have different meaning to different recruits. Perhaps Goffmaa and others have been overimpressed with the degree of humiliation and profanation of self that occurs in certain organisations. Even in the harshest of institutional settings, some recruits will undergo a brutal divestiture process with a calculated indifference and stoic nonchalance. Some recruits too will have been through divestiture processes so frequently that new socialisation attempts can be undergone rather matter-of-factly. Furthermore, "total institutions" sometimes offer a recruit a sort of home-away-from-home that more or less complements the recruit's entering self-image. In such situations, one's preinstitutional identity can be sustained, if not enhanced, with ease.

Yet, the fact remains that many organisations consciously promote ordeals designed to make the recruit whatever the organisation deems appropriate, what Schein has described as "up-ending" experiences. In extreme circumstances, recruits are forced to abstain from certain types of behaviour, must publicly degrade themselves and others, and must follow a rigid set of rules and regulations. This process, when voluntarily undergone, serves to commit and bind the person to the organisation and is typically premised upon a strong desire on the part of the recruit to become an accepted member of the organisation. In brief, the recruit's entrance into the role or system is aided by his or her "awe" of the institution and this "awe" then sustains the individual's motivation through subsequent ordeals of divestiture. Consider here, first year law students at elite universities or young women entering religious orders.

There are many familiar illustrations of organisations in this society that require a recruit to pass robust tests in order to gain privledged access into their realms: religious cults, elite law schools, self-realisation groups, professional athletic teams, many law enforcement agencies, military organisations, and so on. Even some business occupations such as certified public accounting have stiff licensing requirements which, to many recruits, appear much like a divestiture process. It should be kept in mind however that these stern tactics provide an identity-bestowing as well as an identity-destroying process. Coercion is not necessarily a damaging assault on the person. Indeed, it can be a device for stimulating many personal changes that are evaluated positively by the person and others. Given these concerns, some propositions can now be presented which seek to further explicate the workings of this socialisation tactic in organisational settings.

For an Individual to have the motivation and strength to be a role innovator, it is necessary for that person to be reinforced individually by various other members of the organisation (which must be an informal process since it implies disloyalty to the role, group, organisational segment, or total organisation Itself), to be free of sequential stages which might inhibit innovative efforts, to be exposed to innovative role models or none at all, and to experience an affirmation of self throughout the process. Therefore, it will probably only occur when an individual who is innovative in orientation at the outset encounters an essentially benign socialisation process which not only does not discourage role innovation, but genuinely encourages it.

REFERENCES

Ash, M.G. (1992). "Cultural Contexts and Scientific Change in Psychology: Kurt Lewin in Iowa." *American Psychologist*, Vol. 47, No. 2, pp. 198-207.

Hatch, M.J., (2006) "Organization Theory: Modern, symbolic, and postmodern perspectives." 2nd Ed. Oxford University Press

Jones, Ishmael, (2008) *The Human Factor: Inside the CIA's Dysfunctional Intelligence Culture.* New York: Encounter Books.

Robbins, Stephen P. (2004) *Organizational Behavior - Concepts, Controversies, Applications.* 4th Ed. Prentice Hall.

10

Psychological Aspects of Team Work

Teams touch our lives everyday and their effectiveness is important to well-being across a wide range of societal functions. There is over 50 years of psychological research—literally thousands of studies—focused on understanding and influencing the processes that underlie team effectiveness. Our goal in this monograph is to sift through this voluminous literature to identify what we know, what we think we know, and what we need to know to improve the effectiveness of work groups and teams.

We begin by defining team effectiveness and establishing the conceptual underpinnings of our approach to understanding it. We then turn to our review, which concentrates primarily on topics that have well-developed theoretical and empirical foundations, to ensure that our conclusions and recommendations are on firm footing. Our review begins by focusing on cognitive, motivational/affective, and behavioural team processes—processes that enable team members to combine their resources to resolve task demands and, in so doing, be effective. We then turn our attention to identifying interventions, or "levers," that can shape or align team processes and thereby provide tools and applications that can improve team effectiveness. Topic-specific conclusions and recommendations are given throughout the review.

Teams of people working together for a common cause touch all our lives. From everyday activities like air travel, fire fighting, and running the United Way drive to amasing feats of human accomplishment like climbing Mt. Everest and reaching for the stars, teams are at the center of how work gets done in modern life. Although how teams function is often beneath the level of everyday awareness, unexpected successes, such as Team USA's winning of the Olympic Gold Medal for Hockey, and failures, such as FEMA's sluggish response to hurricane Katrina, make team functioning and team effectiveness highly salient.

Failures of team leadership, coordination, and communication are well-documented causes of the majority of air crashes, medical errors, and industrial disasters. Our point is simple: teams are central and vital to everything we do in modern life. Our purpose in this monograph is to elucidate what more than 50 years of research on small groups and teams can tell us about the processes that contribute to team effectiveness and, based on that knowledge, to identify leverage points that can be used to make teams more effective.

Organisations around the world are well along a decade-and-a-half evolution in the design of work—shifting from individual jobs in functionalised structures to teams embedded in more complex workflow systems. A variety of forces are driving this shift. Increasing competition, consolidation, and innovation create pressures for skill diversity, high levels of expertise, rapid response, and adaptability. Teams enable these characteristics.

Concomitant with this shift in the organisation of work is the shift in research focus from the study of small interpersonal groups in social psychology to the study of work teams in organisational psychology. This shift in the core of team research was explicitly recognised by Moreland, Hogg, and Hains, who noted the relative decline of group research in social psychology, and by Levine and Moreland, who concluded that small-group research "is alive and well and living elsewhere.

At least seven major reviews of the work-team literature in organisational psychology appeared between 1990 and 2000. More recent reviews of work-team research reflect the emerging perspective of work teams as dynamic, emergent, and adaptive entities embedded in a multilevel system. That is, teams are complex dynamic systems that exist in a context, develop as members interact over time, and evolve and adapt as situational demands unfold.

Dynamic complexity; emergent team processes and phenomena; and development, evolution, and adaptation are key themes that will be reflected in our review. A dynamic, shifting, and complex environment creates commensurate team task demands that members have to resolve though a coordinated process that combines their cognitive, motivational/affective, and behavioural resources. This process is cyclical and reciprocal. When team processes are aligned with environmentally driven task demands, the team is effective; when they are not, the team is not.

We next review the research base to identify critical team processes and emergent states that contribute to team effectiveness. Having established that research foundation, we then consider factors that can influence, shape, and create appropriate team processes.

There has been well over a half century of research in both social psychology and organisational psychology on small groups and teams and related topics. Virtually all of the research papers close with the obligatory acknowledgement that "more research is needed." There is a substantial knowledge base. The real challenge is sifting through this vast literature to isolate those promising team processes that reliably influence team effectiveness and that can also be shaped by deliberate intervention.

First, we sought research topics that were sufficiently mature that they had been the target of one or more meta-analytic reviews. Second, we sought topics that, though not meta-analysed, had been the subject of substantial systematic empirical research. For these areas, our conclusions and recommendations are strong but not unequivocal. Finally, we also considered areas that reflect emerging theory and promising, though not yet extensive, research support. As in any such endeavor, our decisions about what to include and exclude will not please everyone. We offer apologies in advance to all whose work may have been overlooked.

We now begin by articulating our theoretical perspective, as it highlights important themes of our review and its structure. We next review research on team processes and emergent states, giving recommendations about those that are actionable and those that require further development and research attention. If you want to know how to enhance team effectiveness, this is how it can be accomplished.

Nature of Teams and Team Effectiveness

What is a Team?

A team can be defined as (a) two or more individuals who (b) socially interact (c) possess one or more common goals; (d) are brought together to perform organisationally relevant tasks; (e) exhibit interdependencies with respect to workflow, goals, and outcomes; (f) have different roles and responsibilities; and (g) are together embedded in an encompassing organisational system, with boundaries and linkages to the broader system context and task environment.

What is Team Effectiveness?

The conceptualisation of team effectiveness that has shaped the last 40 years of theory and research is based on the logic of an input–process–output (I-P-O) heuristic formulated by McGrath. In this framework, inputs refer to the composition of the team in terms of the constellation of individual characteristics and resources at multiple levels. Processes refer to activities that team members engage in, combining their resources to resolve task demands. Processes thus mediate the translation of inputs to outcomes. Although team processes are by definition dynamic, they are most typically addressed in static terms—as constructs that emerge over time as team members interact and the team develops. Output has three facets:

(a) Performance judged by relevant others external to the team;

(b) Meeting of team-member needs; and (c) viability, or the willingness of members to remain in the team.

These tripartite facets capture the prevalent conceptualisation of team effectiveness. Although McGrath's heuristic is a useful organising framework—it was developed to organise the research literature on small groups circa 1964—it was not intended to be a theory or a formal causal model of team effectiveness. Ithas, nonetheless, been frequently interpreted as a model to be tested.

A Dynamic View of Team Processes and Effectiveness We adopt a more contemporary perspective that has evolved over the last decade, which conceptualises the team as embedded in a multilevel system that has individual, team, and organisational-level aspects; which focuses centrally on task-relevant processes; which incorporates temporal dynamics encompassing episodic tasks and developmental progression; and which views team processes and effectivenessas emergent phenomena unfolding in a proximal task-or social context that teams inpart enact while also being embedded in a larger organisation system or environmental context.

Multilevel System Context

Individual team members comprise the team as a collective entity, an entity that also serves as the social context that influences individual members. Moreover, team members and work teams are embedded in a broader organisational system and task environment that drives the difficulty, complexity, and tempo of the team task. The interactions are reciprocal in that team performance outputs resolve task demands emerging from the surrounding system or environment and change the state of the system or environment in some fashion. These changes can shift unexpectedly and the team must adapt to the changing demands. Thus, it is necessary to understand the system context and linkages across multiple levels—individual, team, organisation—as key sources of contingencies or demands on the team that necessitate aligned team processes.

The degree to which teams are embedded in or tightly linked to the organisational system or a dynamic task environment can vary. As an example, consider a surgical team in the operating room (OR) where what is happening with the patient right now defines the task environment, which then drives team task demands and team-member activity. Relative to the broader organisational-system context the task environment is the primary context in which the OR team is embedded. The situation is similar for aircrews or fire-fighting teams, in which the task environment is the primary embedding context.

For other teams, the broader organisational system is the primary context. A cross-functional project team making a recommendation to management on product development or a top-management team (TMT) revising organisational strategy to meet stiff competition are more tightly included in the organisational system as the primary embedding context.

Team Task

The central focus on what teams have to do—their task—is the key factor that distinguishes a social-psychological perspective on the study of teams, in which the task is merely a means to prompt interpersonal interaction, from an organisational perspective, in which the task is the source of goals, roles, and task-based exchanges. For the latter, interpersonal interaction is relevant, but it is in the background rather than the foreground. First, it sets minimum requirements for the resource pool—the constellation of team-member individual differences and capabilities—that is available across team members. If members collectively lack necessary knowledge, skills, abilities, or resources to resolve the team task, the team cannot be effective. Second, the team task determines the primary focus of team-member activities. Our focus is on teams that primarily do things and that, in the process of striving toward and accomplishing goals, also have to make decisions and create, invent, and adapt solutions to resolve task-driven problems. Thus, the team task determines the workflow structure and coordination demands necessary for accomplishing individual and team goals and resolving task requirements. Team processes as emergent constructs or "states" are a way to capture coordination of team-member effort and factors relevant to it, as well as the alignment of team processes with task demands.

Time

Team processes develop and unfold over time. The extent to which team processes align with task demands is a function of team learning, skill acquisition, and development. Key temporal dimensions include (a) task cycles or episodes that "entrain" the team to task dynamics by making specific, iterative, and repeated demands on team processes and (b) linear development of indeterminate duration across the team's life cycle of formation, development, maintenance, and decline/ dissolution. And, although processes are clearly dynamic, over time stable process constructs, or what Marks et al. call emergent states, develop, providing a means to capture or summarise team processes.

Our Approach

We begin our review by establishing what we know about critical team processes and emergent states and how they contribute to team effectiveness. Our purpose is to identify processes that have well-established, research-based linkages to team effectiveness that therefore should be targets for interventions to improve team functioning. We then highlight research-based interventions that can leverage team processes.

TEAM PROCESSES, EMERGENT STATES AND EFFECTIVENESS

Conceptually, process captures how team members combine their individual resources, coordinating knowledge, skill, and effort to resolve task demands. Team effectiveness is an emergent result that unfolds across levels and over time. This perspective on team processes is clearly dynamic, but it is also the case that the repeated interactions among individuals that constitute processes tend to regularise, such that shared structures and emergent states crystallise and then serve to guide subsequent process interactions. Thus it is important to appreciate that while processes are dynamic and therefore difficult to capture in real time, they yield collective cognitive structures, emergent states, and regular behaviour patterns that have been enacted by, but also guide, team processes.

In that sense, team cognitive structures, emergent states, and routinised behaviour patterns are the echoes of repeated process interactions and, hence, are indicative of the nature and quality of dynamic team processes.

Team Cognitive Processes and Structures Small-group research has a long tradition of studying cognitive constructs such as group norms and role expectations that guide interpersonal interactions among team members. While not denying the importance of interpersonal interactions, research in organisational psychology has tended to address cognitive constructs that are more focused on guiding task-relevant interactions among team members. We focus on a set of team cognitive constructs that represent the structure of collective perception, cognitive structure or knowledge organisation, and knowledge or information acquisition—constructs that have amassed a sufficient research foundation to support their value for enhancing team effectiveness.

Unit and Team Climate

The notion of climate as an interpretation of the group situation or environment can be traced back to early work by Lewin, Lippitt, and White, with much research and development over the intervening decades. Contemporary theory and research regard climate as cognitively based, descriptive, interpretive perceptions of salient features, events, and processes that characterise the "strategic imperatives" of the organisational and team context. Research has established the emergence of collective climates at the organisational level, in smaller units such as bank branches, and within teams embedded in organisations.

There is a large and growing research base demonstrating that collective climate relates to the performance, member satisfaction, and viability facets of individual, team, and unit effectiveness. For example, Schneider and Bowen showed that a shared, collective climate in which service was the salient strategic imperative predicted customers' satisfaction with their bank branch. Anderson and West showed that a team climate for innovation predicted overall team innovativeness, novelty of innovations, and number of innovations. Hofmann and Stetser showed that a team climate for safety predicted safety-related behaviours and actual accident rates in a chemical plant where high-reliability performance is necessarily a high priority.

Moreover, research on both service climate and safety climate has been systematic, developing a set of findings that convincingly demonstrate significant effects on customer perceptions of service quality and increases in safety-related behaviours with corresponding reductions in objective accident indicators, respectively.

As research supporting the utility of collective climates for predicting meaningful organisational, unit, and individual outcomes began to accrue, researchers also began to explore factors that influenced perceptual consensus and the emergence of unit climate. Harkening back to the roots of climate theory, Koslowski and Doherty proposed that leaders shape the interpretation of climate for those team members with whom they have a good leader–member exchange relationship. Their results showed that team members with good LMX relations had climate perceptions that were both similar to their leader and consensual with each other, relative to those with poor LMX relations, whose perceptions were discordant with the leader and each other.

Rentsch, building on Schneider and Reichers' suggestion that social interaction shapes consensual climate, showed that networks of individuals with frequent informal social interactions showed greater consensus on climate relative to consensus within those individuals' formal organisational units. This research demonstrates nicely the theoretical assertion that social interaction contributes to shared climates.

In an effort to better capture climate emergence, Brown, Koslowski, and Hattrup suggested that sharing, consensus, or agreement on climate perceptions ought to be a substantive phenomenon of interest rather than a mere statistical justification for aggregating individual climate perceptions to represent unit climates. Rather than treating the emergence of climate as all or none, they argued that degree of perceptual agreement could be conceptualised as measuring the extent to which climate perceptions were dispersed, had started to converge, or were highly consensual within the unit and therefore the extent to which climate had emerged.

Subsequent work has generated support for this dispersion-theory conceptualisation. For example, Schneider, Salvaggio, and Subirats reported data showing that aggregated individual-level employee perceptions of unit service climate significantly interacted with unit climate strength, thereby demonstrating that greater within-unit consensus or strength yielded stronger relationships between service climate and aggregated customer perceptions of service quality concurrently and over a 3-year time interval. Moreover, climate strength interacted with aggregated innovation climate to influence average unit satisfaction and commitment, and climate strength interacted with aggregated goal orientation to influence average unit commitment.

Based on this systematic body of theory development and empirical support, we conclude that a collective climate that captures the strategic imperatives reflective of the core mission and objectives of an organisation, unit, or team is a key emergent cognitive structure that shapes processes relevant to goals and their accomplishment. We further conclude that factors influencing climate consensus or strength—such as strategic imperatives, leadership, and social interaction—represent leverage points for shaping collective climates to influence team effectiveness.

Team Mental Models and Transactive Memory Team mental models and transactive memory both refer to cognitive structures or knowledge representations that enable team members to organise and acquire information necessary to anticipate and execute actions. As we detail below, team mental models refer to knowledge structures or information held in common, whereas transactive memory refers to knowledge of information distribution within a team. Although these concepts may seem to bear some superficial resemblance to team climate, they are quite distinctive. Where climate tends to be more general in nature, team mental models and transactive memory are more specific to the team task and work system.

Team mental models capture the shared, organised understanding and mental representation of knowledge or beliefs relevant to key elements of the team's task environment. The concept of a mental model developed in the human-factors literature as an expert's cognitive representation of a system that could be used for predicting system states and for generating inferences about system behaviour. We should highlight that the enhancement of coordination has been posed in the context of action teams that perform critical tasks under dynamic uncertainty where coordination is a critical team process. This speculation energised considerable interest and activity in the team-research community.

Four primary content domains of team mental models were originally proposed. They include (a) knowledge about the equipment and tools used by the team; (b) understanding of the team task, including its goals, performance requirements, and problems; (c) awareness of team-member composition and resources, including representations of what individual members know and believe and their skills, preferences, and habits ; and (d) what team members know or believe about appropriate or effective processes.

One of the biggest challenges in research and application centres on how to measure and represent team mental models as group-level cognitive structures. Mohammed et al. identified four techniques, including pathfinder networks multidimensional scaling interactively elicited cause mapping and text-based cause mapping that can be useful for measuring team-level cognitive structure. The evaluation of the strengths and weaknesses of these different techniques by Mohammed et al. was based on seven criteria including the treatment of content, evaluation of structure, a clear standard, reliability evidence, effectiveness, utility for team analyses, and other considerations. They concluded that the decision of which technique to use depends on the research question under examination and on the team context. For example, if researchers know the key concepts of a domain and want to capture the structural relations among concepts then PF and MDS are appropriate because they provide tools to represent, describe, and compare structures. On the other hand, if researchers are interested in measuring team members' belief relations, then IECM and TBCM may be more appropriate because they necessitate the direct elicitation from participants of concepts and relational information that capture the richness of cognitive content.

The presumption of the shared-mental-model literature is that team effectiveness will improve if team members have a shared understanding of the task, team, equipment, and situation. Although the notion of a common or shared team mental model has tended to dominate the research, there is recognition that team mental models may be more complex, in the sense that members do not necessarily have isomorphic knowledge structures but possess some sharing and also some unique structural information that is compatible with that of other member roles. This conceptualisation of networked knowledge incorporates aspects of a distributional model somewhat similar to the notion of transactive memory.

Although there have been some concerns regarding the adequacy of empirical work relative to conceptual development, research has accumulated to provide solid support for the general presumption that shared mental models are associated with team effectiveness. Their results indicated that shared mental models enhanced performance on collective tasks requiring interdependence among team members but did not impact those tasks that could be completed without coordinated actions—which is consistent with the general thesis. Mathieu, Heffner, Goodwin, Salas, and Cannon-Bowers examined the effect of shared mental models on team processes and performance using two-person teams performing a PC-based combat flight simulation.

There has also been theory and research to identify interventions that enhance the development of team mental models. Focusing on leadership, Koslowski and colleagues posited that team leaders could play a key role in shaping team mental models by linking task cycles or episodes to a regulated learning process. Prior to action, the leader helps set team learning goals commensurate with current team capabilities; during action, the leader monitors team performance ; and as the team disengages from action, the leader diagnoses performance deficiencies and guides process feedback. Marks, Saccaro, and Mathieu showed that leader pre-briefs that focused on appropriate team task strategies yielded better team mental models, processes, and performance. Other research focusing on the effects of leader pre-briefs and debriefs has also shown positive effects on team mental models and team performance. Planning, strategies, and contingencies enable teams to overcome obstacles to goal accomplishment, and training that focuses on skills relevant to diagnosis, feedback, and planning is also important.

In addition, there are several training techniques that are effective for shaping the development of team mental models and enhancing team performance. Mental models, in turn, influenced team-communication processes and performance. Moreover, the effects of team mental models and communication processes on team performance were stronger when the task conditions were novel, suggesting that team mental models may help team members adapt to the unexpected. Marks, Sabella, Burke, and Saccaro examined the effects of cross-training on team-interaction mental models and their subsequent effects on coordination, backup behavio, and performance. Their results indicated that cross-training improved team-interaction mental models, assessed via PF, and that the effects of team mental models on team performance were mediated by improved coordination and backup behaviour. Team self-correction training focuses on skills relevant to (a) event review (following a task episode), (b) error identification, (c) feedback exchange, and (d) planning for subsequent task episodes.

Much of this growing empirical support for the efficacy of shared team mental models for fostering team processes and performance has been conducted in the context of action or command-and-control teams—real or simulated—but there is evidence in more recent work that it extends to other types of teams, such as TMTs.

On the basis of this systematic body of theory development and growing empirical support, we conclude that a shared team mental model that captures the structure of relations among key aspects of the team, its task and role system, and its environment is a key emergent cognitive structure that shapes coordination processes relevant to team goals and their accomplishment.

The concept of transactive memory, as a memory system distributed across group members, was first proposed by Wegner to explain why close personal relationships often foster the development of common memory, and much of the formative work on transactive memory has studied it in the context of intimate relationships. From a team perspective, transactive memory is a group-level collective system for encoding, storing, and retrieving information that is distributed across group members.

In that sense, one can conceptualise transactive memory as a network, with team members and their unique knowledge representing nodes with links representing other members' awareness of that unique knowledge. When each team member learns in a general sense what other team members know in detail, the team can draw on the detailed knowledge distributed across members of the collective. The development of transactive memory involves the communication and updating of information members have about the areas of the other members' unique knowledge.

Given the presumed distribution of specialised memories across team members, transactive memory systems should be more cognitively efficient, allowing high specialisation and greater capacity. Conceptually, such systems should reduce the cognitive load on individuals, enlarge the collective pool of expertise, and minimise redundancy. On the other hand, there are likely to be limits to the size of such a distributed memory system, at which point tracking costs may outweigh memory gains. And, there are time lags and efficiency costs for accessing a distributed memory that may be detrimental to team effectiveness in time-critical situations.

Transactive memory is an intriguing concept that augments the focus on shared knowledge that dominates the team-mental-model literature. Unfortunately, however, empirical research on transactive memory is not commensurate with its theoretical development. Moreover, compared to the research base on team mental models, research on team transactive memory is still in its infancy. Members of groups that had trained together evidenced stronger transactive-memory systems specialised for remembering different aspects of the task, they coordinated more effectively, and they showed greater trust in other members' expertise. In addition, transactive memory mediated the effects of group training on task performance. A follow-up study conducted by Moreland used a similar task and design. He used a more direct measure of transactive memory by assessing the complexity of group members' beliefs about other members' expertise, belief accuracy, and agreement about the distribution of expertise within the group.

More recent research has begun to address some of the conceptual and measurement problems identified by Koslowski and Bell that have plagued this literature. Austin, for example, integrated prior research to develop assessments of four dimensions of transactive memory, including (a) knowledge stock as the pool or combination of individual knowledge, (b) consensus about knowledge sources, (c) specialisation of knowledge, and (d) the accuracy of knowledge identification. Examining 27 product teams (N 5 263) in a sporting-goods company, results indicated that both specialisation and accuracy were substantially related to external and internal evaluations of effectiveness and that accuracy was also related to external ratings of goal accomplishment. Lewis, drawing on Moreland, developed a three-dimensional perceptual measure of transactive memory. The dimensions included specialisation, credibility, and coordination—which, although labelled differently, are consistent with Moreland and Austin. The study was rigorous in its development and validation of the assessment method. A related paper that appears to be based on a portion of the same data concluded that frequent face-to-face communication facilitated the formation of transactive-memory systems and that transactive memory was related to team performance and viability.

This recent research is promising, although there is also a need for clear conceptual and empirical demarcations across the team cognitive constructs of climate, mental models, and transactive memory. For example, the assessment approach developed by Lewis, which necessitates within-group perceptual consensus, blurs the distinction between climate, team mental models, and transactive-memory systems. The content of its perceptual dimensions is based on transactive-memory conceptions, but because it incorporates the assumption of shared within-team perceptions to support data aggregation it mirrors assessments of shared team climate and some assessments of shared team mental models. This observation is not meant to suggest that the technique is flawed. Rather, we simply note the need for clear conceptual and empirical demarcations across these team cognitive constructs.

There is merit to both the team-mental-models and transactive-memory approaches, but there are also important conceptual distinctions that may be differentially important for teams under different contingencies. In particular, it is likely that the difference between task interdependence, which necessitates differentiated role specialisation, and pooled tasks, which necessitate more common knowledge, will bear on the importance of knowledge distribution that would make transactive memory more important relative to knowledge sharing that would make shared mental models more relevant.

As research on transactive memory goes forward, there is a need to expand on the formative work that examined its formation, emergence, and effects in work teams. Given the rise of virtual teams, this finding should prompt concerted efforts to understand the reasons for such barriers and to try to develop augmentations for computer-based and other forms of remote communication. Research also shows that common experience or training may be useful for developing transactive-memory systems. Thus, this may be an area in which the use of interpositional cross-training, which has proven useful in the development of shared mental models, may also help to foster the development of better transactive-memory systems.

Team Learning

The concept of group or team learning refers to the acquisition of knowledge, skills, and performance capabilities of an interdependent set of individuals through interaction and experience. Team learning is fundamentally based on individual learning, but when viewed as more than a mere pooling of individual knowledge it can be distinguished as a team-level property that captures the collective knowledge pool, potential synergies among team members, and unique individual contributions. Certainly, the concept of learning is broad enough to be applied to levels of social organisation beyond the individual and it has been so applied. Indeed, the literature on organisational learning has developed over the last four decades into a rich, multifaceted, and multidisciplinary area of inquiry focused on creating, retaining, and transferring knowledge among higher-level entities.

One of the key challenges is to distinguish team learning from related concepts such as team mental models and transactive memory, which also develop through collective interaction and common experience. One way to make such a distinction is to regard team climate, mental models, and transactive memory as emergent states that develop from learning as a dynamic behavioural process of interaction and exchange among team members. When viewed as a process, it becomes more apparent that learning is contextually based and socially bound.

One emerging perspective on collective learning that is consistent with this process view is represented by Edmondson's model of team learning. She noted that much of the relatively limited literature on team learning has been conducted in the laboratory, which limits the nature of the phenomena that can be observed. The key construct in this model is the team perception of psychological safety, a climate-like shared perception that the team is a safe context for interpersonal risk taking. Team psychological safety, in turn, influenced team learning behaviours indicative of a team learning process—such as seeking feedback, sharing information, experimenting, asking for help, and discussing errors—which then influenced team performance.

Because learning, motivation, and performance are entwined, Edmondson's approach to team learning provides a useful linkage with this other emerging work, suggesting the potential for an effective integration in a broader model that will become apparent.

Apart from Edmondson's research, there has been relatively little research on team learning outside of the laboratory. Here we provide a couple of illustrations of lab research on team learning. Group performance—making origami birds—exhibited a performance learning curve, with output increasing significantly at a decreasing rate over six trials. High turnover and high complexity of the task were detrimental to group performance, with the detrimental effect increasing as groups gained experience, suggesting in the case of turnover that aspects of group knowledge were being lost.

Using a complex command-and-control radar simulation and four-person teams, Ellis et al. found that team composition and structure influenced learning. Team learning was assessed as an aggregate of the effectiveness and efficiency with which individual team members took action against unknown radar contacts, where effectiveness and efficiency represented the degree of match between resources expended to take action and the capabilities possessed by a contact. Because each member had some unique information to help identify the type of contact, teams that were more effective and efficient on average could be inferred to have shared information or learned from one another. Teams composed of members with higher average cognitive ability and teams whose workloads were more evenly distributed among members learned more.

Although there is interesting work being conducted on collective knowledge management, it is largely at levels beyond teams and focuses on processes that are more macro in origin and effect. At best, the research on team learning is still in the formative stage and needs improved focus and rigor. First, team learning as an outcome is typically inferred from changes in team performance. It is rarely assessed directly as a construct in its own right. Relatedly, many of the factors having an impact on team learning are also likely to affect team performance via pathways other than learning. It is impossible to disentangle the process pathways and to map the pattern of effects as long as researchers continue to rely on the assumption that teams have learned rather than on direct assessments of team learning. In a related vein, there is some question as to whether team learning as a knowledge-based outcome can be meaningfully distinguished from team mental models and transactive memory.

Second, as we suggested earlier, it may be more valuable to conceptualise team learning as a process that yields shared knowledge, team mental models, and transactive-memory structures as emergent states. However, with the exception of the work conducted by Edmondson, there has been relatively little research to specify the process by which team learning occurs. A process perspective necessitates simultaneous attention to both the individual and team levels of analysis. Researchers would not be able to simply combine disparate individual actions into an aggregate. Rather, they would have to more carefully delineate how disparate individual learning and action emerge as a collective phenomenon.

Team Interpersonal, Motivational, and Affective Processes

Research on processes has a long history in small-group research, with much of that effort traditionally centred on processes that capture motivational tendencies, relations among team members, and affective reactions. These processes imply a dynamic unfolding, but measures of team processes are most often static assessments that fail to capture temporal dynamics. That is why Marks et al. suggest that it is more accurate to describe the construct measures of team processes as emergent states. We will use both terms interchangeably and explicitly acknowledge that these constructs emerge from dynamic interactions among team members that tend to stabilise over time.

Team Cohesion

Group cohesion is one of the earliest and most widely studied team-process characteristics. Team researchers have offered multiple definitions of cohesion. Festinger defined cohesiveness as ''the resultant of all the forces acting on the members to remain in the group''. Festinger is also responsible for suggesting the three facets that comprise cohesion—member attraction, group activities, and prestige or group pride—although early researchers tended to view cohesion as a unitary construct. Nonetheless, other researchers have often emphasised only one of the facets. Carron defined cohesiveness as a process that reflects a group's tendency to stick together and remain united to reach a common goal. Goodman, Ravlin, and Schminke defined cohesiveness as the commitment of members to the group's task.

These somewhat mixed definitions or emphases are reflected in different conceptualisations of the dimensionality of group cohesion.

Gross and Martin described cohesiveness in terms of two underlying dimensions: task cohesiveness and interpersonal cohesiveness. Task cohesiveness is defined as a group's shared commitment or attraction to the group task or goal. Interpersonal cohesiveness is defined as the group members' attraction to or liking of the group. Interpersonal cohesiveness allows groups to have less inhibited communication and to effectively coordinate their efforts. Indeed, a recent meta-analysis by Beal, Cohen, Burke, & McLendon found that it has been largely neglected in over 50 years of research, although it contributes to team effectiveness at levels comparable to the other cohesion facets— but we are getting ahead of the story.

Research has generally supported a positive relationship between team cohesion and performance. For example, Smith et al. found that the level of cohesiveness in top-management teams was positively related to return on investment and sales growth. Similar results in top-management teams have been found by Hambrick and Katsenbach and Smith. Moreover, several meta-analytic reviews conducted over the last 15 years have consistently supported a positive relationship between cohesion and group performance. An early meta-analytic review by Evans and Dion that focused solely on group-level cohesion and group performance concluded that the relationship is positive, although their study was based on only 18 effect sizes; they reported a wide confidence interval; and they did not examine moderators, even though sampling error accounted for only 64% of effect-size variance.

A more comprehensive meta-analysis by Mullen and Cooper also concluded that cohesion is significantly related to performance in a variety of teams, with an overall effect size of r 5.248. To their credit, the Mullen and Cooper review examined the effects of several moderators of the relationship, including requirements for member interaction, cohesion dimensions, study setting and the effects of time. Of interest, they did not find significant effects for interaction requirements, suggesting that the relationship between cohesion and performance was not influenced by the extent to which members had to coordinate their knowledge and skills or could essentially work alone.

Unfortunately, as detailed in an incisive conceptual analysis by Gully, Devine, and Whitney, both the Evans and Dion and Mullen and Cooper reviews suffer from serious limitations that make interpretation of their meta-analytic estimates problematic. In particular, the reviews confound team task interdependence and levels of analysis. With respect to levels of analysis, the problem is one of misspecification by mixing data at the individual level with team-level data but drawing conclusions at the team level. There are strong conceptual distinctions between cohesion as an individual perception and cohesion as a shared perception among members. Moreover, this confound is not merely a conceptual problem.

Unlike the prior reviews, Gully et al. distinguished between research that examined cohesion appropriately at the team level of analysis, where theory predicts that the relationship should be stronger, and studies that measured cohesion at the individual level, which is a conceptual misspecification that should yield weaker relationships. They also examined task interdependence as a moderator.

Their meta-analysis yielded an overall effect size of r 5.265 with a confidence interval ranging from.211 to.318. Sampling error accounted for 64% of the effect-size variance. These findings for the overall effects, which mix team- and individual-level studies, are comparable to those reported by Mullen and Cooper. At the individual level, the cohesion–performance relationship was.228 with a confidence interval ranging from.176 to.281. Sampling error accounted for 98% of the effect-size variance. For the team-level relationship, the effect size was.317 with a confidence interval ranging from.231 to.401. Sampling error accounted for 60% of the effect-size variance. As expected, the relationship at the team level was stronger, with relatively little overlap in the two confidence intervals. In addition, task interdependence was also a moderator. Sampling error accounted for 96% of the effect-size variance. This work by Gully and colleagues represents an incisive conceptual analysis and rigorous meta-analysis of the cohesion–performance relationship. Moreover, their differential findings for levels of analysis and team task interdependence are consistent with our emphasis on the importance of these characteristics with respect to understanding team effectiveness.

More recently, Beal et al. also meta-analytically reviewed the relationship between group cohesion and performance. In many ways, their analysis was a refinement of the Gully et al. review. First, based on the Gully et al. findings, they only examined research that appropriately treated the relationship at the team level and they also examined task interdependence as a moderator. Second, they carefully distinguished the three types of cohesion—interpersonal cohesiveness, task cohesiveness, and group pride—and performance criteria. They also distinguished whether outcomes were adjusted for inputs or not arguing that efficiency measures are more indicative of team performance.

As expected, their analysis revealed that group cohesion was more strongly related to performance behaviours than to outcomes and was more strongly related to efficiency than to effectiveness measures. The mean corrected correlation between cohesion and performance behaviours was.301, whereas the mean corrected correlation between cohesion and performance outcomes was.168, a difference that was statistically significant.

In contrast to the findings reported by Mullen and Cooper, Beal et al. found that all three components of cohesion were significant and, although varying in magnitude, did not differ significantly from each other. The effect sizes were.199 for interpersonal cohesion,.261 for group pride, and.278 for task commitment. Resolution of that issue necessitates a larger base of primary research that incorporates all three facets. Finally, as would be expected, the magnitude of the relations between the cohesion components and the different performance criteria paralleled the overall findings described above, with stronger relations exhibited for behaviour and efficiency measures.

The meta-analyses conducted by Gully et al. and Beal et al. have done much to clarify the relationship between the components of team cohesion and team performance. All of the cohesion components are significantly related to team performance at the team level of analysis, with task commitment and group pride exhibiting the strongest relations. Cohesion is more strongly related to what team members do than to team outcomes, but both relations are significant. And, as one would expect, team cohesion is more strongly related to team performance when the team task has a more complex workflow, thereby making team members more interdependent and placing more emphasis on team-member coordination.

On the other hand, research has relatively little to reveal regarding the antecedents of team cohesion. One could speculate that the composition of the team in terms of member personalities may be important. Barrick, Stewart, Neubert, and Mount, for example, found that teams high in extraversion and emotional stability had higher levels of social cohesion. Clear norms and goals may help a team to develop both task and interpersonal cohesion. However, it is difficult to know the direction of this relationship.

In summary, the research foundation for team cohesion is sufficiently well developed to conclude that it is an emergent affective state that is related to team performance and that the relationship strengthens as team workflow demands increase interdependence and require greater coordination of information and effort. On that basis, we conclude that teams with greater collective task and interpersonal cohesion and pride will be more effective. However, the research base to help identify techniques for enhancing group cohesion is as yet not sufficiently developed to warrant specific recommendations for how to develop these desirable emergent states. This is an obvious target for research.

Team Efficacy and Group Potency

Self-efficacy is an individual's appraisal of his or her task-specific capability to achieve a particular level of performance in goal accomplishment. Self-efficacy is central in social-cognitive theory. As individuals direct action in the pursuit of goals, they monitor progress through feedback and reflect on discrepancies between current performance and their goals. To the extent that perceptions of progress are adequate, their appraisals of self-efficacy build. Self-efficacy is important because it leads to setting higher level goals when initial goal levels are accomplished, it boosts persistence when goals are difficult and challenging, and it fosters adaptation to increasing task complexity. Meta-analytic findings at the individual level of analysis have shown that self-efficacy is significantly related to performance. Given these findings for the important role of self-efficacy in individual effort and performance, parallel concepts of team efficacy and collective efficacy have been proposed, as has the related but distinct concept of group potency.

Self and team efficacy are distinct in that the collective construct represents a group or team-level property that is shared, consensual, and held in common across group members and may be distinct from individuals' own self-perceptions of competence. It is not a simple aggregate of self-efficacy across group members; rather, it references the team as the collective entity with respect to shared perceptions. Similar to self-efficacy, collective efficacy is hypothesised to influence what a group chooses to do how much effort it will exert, and its persistence in the face of failure.

Shea and Gusso defined group potency as a generalised collective belief that the group can be effective. Although many researchers view team efficacy and group potency as very similar constructs, they are distinct in that collective efficacy is task specific and group potency is a shared group-level belief about its general effectiveness across multiple tasks and contexts. Moreover, meta-analytic findings indicate distinctive moderator effects across the two constructs.

Empirical support for the positive effects of team efficacy and team potency on team performance is substantial. Much of the supporting experimental research involves ad hoc teams performing simulated tasks. Although the generalisability of this research is often questioned because of the use of student samples, simple tasks, and the relatively short duration of the studies, some of this work involves simulations of complex tasks that entail higher levels of interdependence, greater demands for coordination, and more psychological fidelity with their real-world counterparts.

A recent meta-analysis by Gully et al. reported a significant mean corrected correlation between team-level efficacy and team performance of.41 and a significant mean corrected correlation of.37 between team-level potency and team performance. In addition, their analysis showed that team efficacy is more likely to be a critical aspect of team processes when interdependence is higher. That is, when interdependence is low, team members essentially make contributions as individuals that are pooled to represent team performance whereas when interdependence is high, team members are more likely to share goals, effort, strategy, and efficacy and team-level efficacy is a more important contributor to team performance. As a more general construct, group potency did not evidence moderation by team interdependence in its relationship to team performance.

Given the well-supported relationship between team efficacy and team performance, there is a clear interest in understanding the antecedent factors that help to promote its development. However, most research has examined the team efficacy–performance relationship, with far less attention devoted to the antecedents of team efficacy, making it difficult to provide direct recommendations about the ways in which managers and organisations can build efficacy at the team level.

Some scholars suggest that antecedents that influence the development of self-efficacy may have a similar role to play, albeit at the team level. Extrapolating from self-efficacy, it has been suggested that teams that are exposed to difficult challenges they can master, that have opportunities to observe effective and ineffective teams, and that are persuaded that they can persist and succeed are more likely to develop team efficacy.

At the team level, collective efficacy is more likely to develop when team members are more interdependent and interactive and have to coordinate task processes, as shared experiences provide a basis for the development of shared perceptions of collective efficacy. Similarly, one would expect that teams composed of learning-oriented members would be more likely to develop team efficacy than would teams composed of performance-oriented members. Thus, we can also assume that team-level goal orientation may be an emergent state rather than a composition characteristic and that team goal orientation is distinct relative to the pattern of individual traits.

Theory and research suggest that team efficacy can be developed by the action of leaders, who can shape team experiences and interactions, and by different forms of team training. For example, Koslowski and colleagues have proposed prescriptive models of team leadership. A key role of leaders in these theoretical frameworks is to create mastery experiences in order to give team members an opportunity to build self-efficacy, and then to shift the focus of members toward the team and shape collective experiences so the team can build collective efficacy. We will address how leaders can develop team efficacy in more detail at the conclusion of the paper. We will also address training in more detail later. Just to illustrate its potential, however, an interesting experiment by Brown provides a good example of how persuasion can be harnessed to build collective efficacy.

With respect to research issues, we believe that further attention to levels-of-analysis concerns; the role of team efficacy in a broader conception of team learning, motivation, and performance processes; and greater attention to the antecedents of team or collective efficacy are warranted. First, team or collective efficacy is distinct from self-efficacy. They have different antecedents and consequences at different levels of analysis. Moreover, the strength of the relationship of team efficacy with team performance is stronger depending on whether it has been conceptualised at the team level or at the individual level. Thus, team and collective efficacy should be appropriately assessed and composed to the team level. That is, items assessing team efficacy should reference the team, not an individual perspective. Moreover, team efficacy as a shared perception should be explicitly evaluated prior to aggregation to the team level. In other words, we assert that team or collective efficacy should be treated as a reference-shift aggregation model rather than as an additive or direct consensus model and recommend that a statistical evaluation be used to justify aggregation using well-established techniques.

Second, the research base demonstrates that team efficacy is an important contributor to team performance. However, team efficacy is but one key emergent state in the broader phenomenon of team learning, motivation, and performance. The supportive findings for team efficacy likely stem from its role in the regulation of attention and effort in the team context. Recent research has validated a homologous multilevel model of individual and team regulation, indicating that team efficacy plays an analogous role to self-efficacy in action initiation and control at the team level.

In summary, the research foundation for team efficacy is sufficiently well developed to conclude that it is an emergent motivational process or state that is related to team performance, and that the relationship strengthens as team workflow demands require greater coordination of information and effort. Based on the meta-analytic findings, group potency as a more global assessment of team capabilities also evidences a meaningful relationship with team performance. We conclude that factors influencing the development of self-efficacy can be adapted to develop team efficacy and potency. In particular, we believe that team leadership and teamtraining interventions are leverage points for shaping the development of team efficacy and potency. We also acknowledge that additional research is needed in this promising area of intervention.

Team Affect, Mood, and Emotion

In their review on affect in the workplace, Brief and Weiss differentiate among affect, moods, and emotions. All three involve good or bad feelings, but they differ in specificity, duration, and the target of the feelings. Emotions have specific affective characteristics, exist for a finite period of time, and evoke particular behaviours and biological responses directed toward specific identifiable objects. Moods also evoke feelings with specific identifiable characteristics, but they last longer and the targets and feelings are more diffuse.

As we examine this area of literature, there are a couple of issues relating to precision of terminology and the proximity of effects that warrant attention. First, the literature on team-level feelings also refers to emotions, moods, and affect. However, this literature is far less precise in its distinction among these feelings-oriented constructs. ''Emotion'' often is the preferred term for team-level affective states in spite of the fact that emotions rarely or ever refer to feelings that are narrowly focused. As we describe this area of work, we will be specific with respect to the authors' terminology, asking readers to keep in mind that they often may not be labeling their affective-state construct with the precision of Brief and Weiss. For our part, we will use the term affect when referring to feelings. Second, it is also worth noting that the potential effects on team effectiveness of team affect, mood, and emotion are likely to be more distil than emergent states that are more specific and proximal. The latter concepts are, in a sense, behaviourally defined scripts more proximal to team outcomes like performance and more focused on a specific set of behaviours than are the more distil concepts of mood, emotions, and affect.

The effects of team affect have been investigated both in terms of the team- or mean level of affect and the dispersion of affect across team members. In almost all cases, the effects of team-level affect are addressed with respect to its impact on team members' cognitions, behaviour, or other affective characteristics. Barsade and her colleagues refer to these as "top-down" effects. George, for example, assessed the positive and negative affectivity (PA and NA) of team members and then examined the relationship between individual members' PA and NA and their teams' mean PA and NA with the members' individual affect score removed. There was a positive correlation between the individual and team scores for both PA and NA, implying that the overall affect level of the team influenced that of the individual team members. She also found team NA negatively related to the level of prosocial behaviour in the teams. Finally, PA was negatively correlated with absences in the teams. George found that the impact of team-level affect was moderated by the similarity among team members on the affect variable as well as on the mean level. When there was within-group agreement on group affective tone, either positive or negative affective tone influenced organisational spontaneity and absenteeism. This finding is indicative of the well-established principle in multilevel theory that within-group agreement, homogeneity, or sharing is essential for the aggregation of facets measured at the individual level to have meaning at the group level. In multilevel theory, these types of findings are regarded as evidence for a contextual effect—the collective characteristic creates a context that influences individual responses—suggesting that team affect creates a situation that influences individual affect in a top-down fashion.

Taking a somewhat different perspective on dispersion, Barsade et al. examined the fit between individual affect and collective affect for TMTs. In a sample of 62 chief executive officers (CEOs) and 239 of their top managers, they found that the more individuals' positive affectivity fit with that of the team, the more positive their attitudes were about group relations and their own influence in the team. Indexing within-team diversity on positive affectivity by the average Euclidian distance among members they found that greater diversity was associated with less use of participatory decision making by the CEO and with lower firm financial performance. When fit was also associated with higher mean levels of positive affectivity, reported levels of team task conflict were lower. Negative affectivity was unrelated to any of the criteria.

Another way to think about dispersion focuses on within-team conflict. High conflict indicates variance among members that may create negative affect. Higher levels of intrateam conflict were associated with greater turnover in a laboratory study. Intrateam conflict is typically seen as the opposite of cohesion. They found destructive conflict styles negatively correlated with task and social cohesion and positively correlated with the frequency of positive conflict.

Three general processes are believed to influence the way that affective states develop in teams: attraction-selection-attrition, which is a combination of bottom-up and top-down processes; contagion, which is bottom-up; and contextual influences, which are top-down. George suggested that team affect develops over time as a result of an ASA process theory that describes how organisations may become more homogeneous over time. Over time, those more similar to others in the team are more likely to remain with the team and those who are more dissimilar are more likely to leave. The result is that, over time, a team should move toward homogeneity on affective constructs. George argued and found that individual team members' PA and NA correlated more highly over time with team-level PA and NAwhen the individual in question was removed from the calculation of team-level PA and NA.

A second process for the development of team-level affect is contagion. Emotional contagion occurs when the emotions and moods of one person are transferred to other proximal individuals. In a nicely controlled laboratory study, Barsade investigated the effect of emotional contagion on team process and performance. The research involved using a confederate trained to express either positive or negative affect and to do so either with strong or weak commitment. Well-designed method checks supported the confederate's successful manipulation of emotions through verbal and facial expression. No effect for level of commitment was found. Confederate behaviour did lead to group-level changes in affect—that is, to "emotional" contagion, both for positive and negative affect. In other words, contagion occurred regardless of whether expressed affect was positive or negative. On the other hand, positive-emotional-contagion group members improved cooperation, decreased conflict, and increased perceived performance; there were no effects of negative contagion on perceptions or behaviour.

Contextual features of the team or its environment provide a third source influencing the development of team affect, mood, or emotions. For example, intergroup conflict resulting from competition and external threat creates within-group homogeneity of feelings and affect toward the in-group and out-group. The simple intervention of requiring teams to hold a discussion on a particular topic created greater polarisation in teams given a positive mood induction prior to discussion, but not in those teams that experienced a negative mood induction. Thus the top-down effect of mood was moderated by the eam problem context—that of discussing the problem.

In summary, research in the area of collective affect, mood, and emotions in work teams is in its infancy, both conceptually and empirically. Conceptually, the rising tide of interest in feeling-focused constructs at the individual level is just beginning to flow to teams. Some of this work shows promise; for much of the rest of it, we must wait and see. At this juncture, we recommend continued research to develop the constructs as meaningful team-level phenomena. However, the research base is not sufficiently well developed to provide guidance for application recommendations.

With respect to team outcomes, the most consistent findings relate more strongly to factors relevant to bonding members to the team than to factors influencing team performance. Prosocial behaviour, citizenship behaviours, and the reduction of turnover were associated with affective characteristics. Moreover, when affect was further divided into positive and negative affectivity, the strength of the impact was greater for the positive affectivity. Given our focus on teams embedded in organisations with a past, present, and future, where affective bonds with team members and the team as a unit develop over time, these affective states are likely to play important roles.

Finally, although affect, moods, and emotions are just beginning to be studied in their own right with respect to teams, they permeate a number of well-established team constructs, particularly cohesion and conflict. Team cohesion and conflict are more targeted concepts that are proximal in a causal chain to critical team outcomes. Thus, the proximal factors of team cohesion and conflict may mediate the relationship between the distil factors of affect, moods, and emotions and team outcomes. Thus, the relative contribution and mechanisms for shared effects are relatively uncharted. Greater integration between the two literatures should be a fruitful avenue for future research that endeavors to build a more solid empirical foundation to capture antecedents and effects.

Team Conflict

The team cognitive and affective processes we have reviewed thus far are largely shared phenomena and have positive relationships with team performance. However, anyone with any experience in work groups or teams knows that things are not always so neat, consensual, and convergent. Conflict and divisiveness are common phenomena in teams and organisations. Theoretical perspectives on team conflict, however, have been, well, conflicting. One perspective views rifts or ''faultlines'' that fracture teams as undermining team-member satisfaction and hindering performance.

On the other hand, other research and theory suggest that conflict is not monolithic and that not all conflict is bad. Conflict can be functional and contribute positively to team performance to the extent that it is moderate; focuses on task-relevant issues; and reveals different points of view, important information, or methods and solutions to problems. This perspective underlies approaches for minimising group-think and the presumed advantages of diversity—that it enhances different perspectives—on team innovation and decision quality. In contrast, when conflict is focused on interpersonal relations and factors not related to the task, it interferes with group information processing and undermines team satisfaction and performance. This perspective—that conflict can be beneficial—is a thread running through several lines of work.

References

Scott, W. Richard. (2007) *Organizations and Organizing: Rational, Natural, and Open Systems Perspectives.* Pearson Prentice Hall.

Weick, Karl E. (1979)*The Social Psychology of Organizing* 2nd Ed. McGraw Hill.

11

Role of Work Psychologists

The growth of work and organisational (W &O) psychology has proved to be different from other specialties. Until the early sixties the growth of W&O psychology was more or less the same as for psychology in general. But in the latter part of the sixties growth started to lag. Students were reluctant to choose this field of specialisation preferring clinical, social and developmental psychology. In society in general industrial organisations were not popular; psychologists working in such organisations were often depicted as "lackeys of management". The stagnation in growth was serious. After 1980 growth became exponential. Interest in clinical and developmental psychology decreased and a rapid growth in interest was seen among students for W&O psychology.

W&O psychologists not only perform certain duties but also that they themselves and the people with whom they collaborate have certain ideas about how a person should behave in a certain position. The focal person has ideas about his/her conduct, and the members of the role set have expectations as to how someone should behave in certain situations. Roles have to do with views and expectations, about rights and obligations and rewards. They are closely related to the way one defines reality, and how one perceives his/her own position. There is continuous interaction between a person who fulfils a role (the focal person) and his/her social environment (the role senders). In such interactions opinions, beliefs and expectations about one another are shaped. Role senders can send opinions which are incompatible with those of other role senders or those of the focal person. This creates role conflict. They can also send ambiguous information which creates role ambiguity. Yet it is in such interaction processes that roles are shaped and accommodated to new developments. Roles are not static. It is within the continuous process of interaction that roles are developed and adapted.

Roles have an individual and collective aspect. The interactive processes have to do with a particular individual in a particular position and lead to the definition of that person's role. But there are also collective aspects, e.g when a person is a member of a profession such a person is not only seen as an individual but also as a representative of that profession. Not only a focal person but also his/her social environment, hold views on how professionals should behave and what they can expect from their social environment.

In society in general there are opinions, beliefs and expectations held about W&O psychologists. Such opinions are held not only by W&O psychologists, but also by the role senders. Opinions have to do with the tasks W&O psychologists perform, and the way they interact with clients. Again these opinions are not static. During continuous interactive processes these opinions are shaped and adapted.

Professional associations have made rules which prescribe how psychologists should act in particular situations. In this way important aspects of the role of the psychologist are defined. This does not mean however that all aspects are defined. A code of conduct is meant to regulate the behaviour of the members of the profession; it also points out what in potential conflict situations the rights and the obligations are of the professionals but also of their clients and other parties. This enables arbitration of conflicts. Parties who feel themselves to be treated unfairly can file complaints. Associations have appointed special committees to handle such complaints. Roles however possess more aspects than are covered in the code of conduct. Important aspects are those which have to do with the domain of the profession and the relationship with the client. When the number of W&O psychologists increases one may expect that this will have consequences regarding the roles they play in society.

Professional Development

At the beginning of the twentieth century W&O psychology was a field with only a small number of pioneers who were very active and had visionary ideas about what W&O psychology could mean to society. One of their most pressing problems was to get the subject as such accepted in society, particularly in universities. Sehönpflug gives a vivid account of the problems and particularly how difficult it was to get cooperation from philosophers in order to establish chairs in psychology.The problems experienced in the middle of the century were completely different ones. At that time it was important to enlarge the knowledge base of the subject and to build research departments. Today the situation has changed once again. The number of professionals is high. Every year thousands of publications appear.

An author writing about the psychologist's role should be aware of cultural differences and differences in social economic systems. In scientific studies such differences do not usually play a major role. Yet roles have to do with norms and values, so role interpretation can differ from one country to another. Laws, i.e. law interpretation and law enforcement in different countries, are not the same. There are many examples where this has an impact on the psychologist's role. For example psychologists in personnel selection in the USA have to work with the extensive regulations on equal opportunity. This has had consequences for selection procedures which have often been subject to scrutiny in court sessions and had to be defended in litigation processes.

For individuals, offering their services to clients, it is attractive to become a member of a profession. As a member of a profession one can profit from the behavioural patterns, opinions and expectations which have been formed in the past. Any individual, confronted with a health problem, knows how to go about consulting a physician. They have developed what Schank and Abelson call "scripts". This being how to consult one's general practitioner. Due to such scripts they know how to find a general practitioner, even when they are not in familiar surroundings; they know how to expect their practitioner to behave, e.g. in using a stethoscope and prescribing drugs. Such scripts facilitate the access to and the interaction with the professional; they are highly helpful, both for the practitioner and the client.

A service provider who is not able to make use of such a script has to invest an enormous amount of effort in contacting clients and explaining the nature of the services he/she has to offer. Clients using a script might never have seen the service provider before, whereas he/

she still has a good idea about what to expect. For the medical profession there are welldeveloped scripts; for most other professions scripts have been developed to a lesser extent. Either the number of clients who are familiar with the service provider is smaller or the clients know less about the service provider.

For W&O psychologists there are clients who possess extensive experience, e.g. for personnel selection and training but there are many clients who have none at all. But even when the usefulness is more limited it can still be very attractive for someone providing personnel selection services to advertise himself or herself as a W&O psychologist. Another reason for the attraction of being a member ofa profession is the recognition it brings. Some services may only be carried out by recognised professionals. Access to clients is restricted to those who are recognised either by law, or by the profession. Employers may require that applicants be a member of a profession. The membership of a profession can also provide necessary prestige to individuals.

While it can be profitable to belong to a profession one also has to pay a price. The profession guarantees, implicitly or explicitly, that their members will serve clients well and this implies a degree of surveillance. A service provider who does not behave in accordance with the values of the profession damages the interests of the said profession. Professions usually have a code of conduct, and explicit roles as to how members should behave in certain situations. Clients who feel that a professional person has not observed such rules can file complaints. There is usually a special committee dealing with such complaints. The most severe sanction is being expelled from membership and losing the right to practise.

There are other forms of surveillance which are less formal. Colleagues are important role senders. There are many ways to let colleagues know how they are expected to behave and to appeal to a person's adherence to norms and values which are considered to be of importance to the profession. Those who behave well and contribute to the profession might be invited to take up positions in the profession and will gain prestige and influence. Those who are seen as not acting in accordance with the values might be excluded from such positions.

So being a member of a profession has its benefits, but also its price. Furthermore professional associations usually impose a substantial fee. This might discourage individuals from becoming a member. Such is the case for many young W&O psychologists who have found employment in organisations where gaining access to clients does not form a major problem for them. Here they might perceive it themselves as being a psychologist without the need for becoming a member of a professional association. This loosens the ties with the profession and it may even occur that such ties are broken. An example could be a person who has graduated in psychology but decided to advertise himself as an organisational consultant or a personnel officer.

Today's W&O profession is differ from that of the past particularly due to exponential growth, a different situation has come into existence. In traditional literature the professional is seen as a service provider one who works for individual clients and does so his whole career. Examples are physicians and public notaries. The situation with W&O psychologists is, however, different. A large majority of W&O psychologists are not selfemployed but are employed by organisations. And in such organisations many psychologists do not work with individuals, e.g. interviewing applicants but have other duties such as developing training programmcs. The argument that the profession provides access to clients is nowadays not valid for many W &O psychologists. Instead of colleague surveillance one is subjected to supervision by the organisation. The professional culture has lost its importance since such psychologists will orientate themselves more towards the organisation by whom they are employed and less so towards the profession. A substantial number of similar psychologists will no longer become a member of the professional association.

This is even more the case since of late many new graduates take up positions which can also be filled by non-psychologists. Due to the enormous growth in the number of graduates, for most of them it is not possible to find employment in typical W&O positions, e.g. personnel selection. So they seek employment elsewhere in other positions. Nowadays there is a strong growth in new service positions for which there are no special training programmes available. Organisations hire university graduates and provide their own special training programmes. So the traditional profession has undergone a change. There are many W&O psychology graduates but there is less interaction between W&O graduates.

DOMAIN OF W&O PSYCHOLOGY

In the past decades the domain of W&O psychology has become strongly differentiated. For a long time personnel selection was the core of the domain. In some European countries W&O psychology and selection were for the general public identical. Many individuals had at one time taken part in psychological test procedures and had become familiar with paper and pencil tests. Conscripts were required to complete psychological tests when drafted into the military forces. So testing was a familiar subject.

The psychologists who worked as professionals in this field had much in common. The domain could be well defended. Psychologists could convince organisations that they had more expertise in the field than any other profession. Clients were convinced that the services had added volume. Others who tried to provide such services could be labelled as quacks. In the early period there were other services as well, e.g. research into safety measures, monotonous work, and leadership but this was less prominent than the work in personnel selection.

Particularly in the past twenty-five years the domain has been broadened and it seems that this differentiation process is set to continue. In this respect marked differences can be seen between countries. The differentiation process started early on in the US and somewhat later in Europe. In the Netherlands there has been a strong interest shown in organisational psychology while in France the interest has been minimal. In 1965 the American Psychologist published guidelines for the training of W&O psychologists. These guidelines described the core of the domain. Three areas are pinpointed: personnel psychology, human factor psychology and industrial social psychology (the latter became organisational psychology in later years). To this core were added: industrial clinical psychology and marketing psychology. In the same year Guion described the domain more or less similarly: engineering psychology, military psychology, consumer psychology, personnel psychology and industrial social psychology.

More recently ENOP, a network of European professors in W&O psychology has set up a reference model for W&O psychologists. This model also describes the core of the domain: personnel psychology, organisational psychology and work psychology. For each of these areas subjects are mentioned e.g. work psychology includes ergonomics, work and health, and stress management. ENOP points out that there are related specialties. These are areas where W&O psychologists are working but which apparently do not belong to the core. Examples are engineering psychology, traffic psychology, managerial psychology, consumer psychology and health psychology. These are areas where others are also active.

The differentiation process can lead to a breaking away of parts of the domain. An area may become more or less independent. Consumer psychology is an example. Guion includes it in his description of the domain but in the ENOP description it is a related specialty. Similarly engineering psychology appears to have become an independent area. Psychologists working in this area have started creating their own divisions in psychological associations.

The above description of the domain points out areas and sub-spccialisations. There are also descriptions on the content. De Wolff put together a directory of W&O psychologists working in European Universities, including the research topics of departments and individuals. There were 91 departments and 390 individuals included. The subjects most frequently mentioned were ergonomics, stress, work satisfaction, automation, functioning of groups, task design, training, selection, organisational structure and organisational development.

Organisations are continually confronted with new demands and that psychologists can help with finding the answers. Interesting in this approach is the description of the domain in terns of interaction between the client needs and the knowledge domain. On looking through textbooks used for the training of W&O psychologists it strikes one that chapter titles used more than 60 years ago are still pretty much the same as those used today. Vitcles mentions individual differences, selection, job analysis, interviewing, safety training, industrial fatigue, motivation, maladjusted workers, problems of supervision and management. Also these days such subjects belong to the core of the domain. From these descriptions one can see that there is continuity as well as development. There are subjects which receive attention over very long periods, like personnel selection. Other subjects have become more independent and valid for all subjects it is the fact that there is additional new knowledge and an adaptation to new demands.

Description of the domain may also serve thc legitimising process. They may mean to inform clients on what to expect from W&O psychologists. Guion feels that W&O Psychology should concern itself with !he relationship between humans and the world of work and more in particular with the adaptation of humans to the workplace and the people with whom they work and what they do to make a living. He mentions three subjects which he feels are essential: "identification of behavioural components and consequences of work performance", "identification and utilisation of talent and determination of the meaning of work".

The Netherlands institute of Psvchologists asked a committee to write a report on professional activities and the training of psychologists in the 21st century. In the report the authors state that the central issue is that humans have to adapt themselves to the everchanging environment. Particularly, technological developments have had a great impact of the task environment. Psychologists will have to assist people in this process of adaptation to new technology and in the creation of a technological environment on a human scale. Three types of interventions are proposed:

> "restructuring the environment", "improving a coping repertoire through Teaming new knowledge and skills", and "building up protection against stress". W&O psychologists state all kind of goals. Goals commonly mentioned are improving effectiveness of behaviour and improving productivity. Another issue often mentioned is human dignity. Goals point out on what issues W&O psychologists should concentrate. These contribute to the dynamic nature of the domain.

There are issues that may become a specialisation in themselves, like ergonomics and consumer psychology. Because the domain is broad it is also more difficult to defend. One of the advantages of specialisation and differentiation could be that the members of the new specialty will do more about the defending of their part of the domain.

It has already been described how the domain develops but this did not fully take into account the rapid growth. The number of W&O psychologists taking up non-psychologists' positions is on the increase. There are now numerous positions for which there is no specific university training programme available, but where employers feel that the W&O psychology training programme provides a good start. W&O psychologists taking up such positions, do, often after some time, no longer identify with W&O psychology.

So it appears that there are three domains of W&O psychology which overlap, but that also have specific elements. The first domain is the one of the researchers. They usually work at universities. Besides doing research they also occupy themselves with teaching, either of W&O students or others. This domain is highly exclusive. To become a researcher at the university one has to be a qualified W&O psychologist. This domain is strongly defended.

Applicants have to present a list of publications, preferably having appeared in international journals of high repute. Further researchers who want to publish articles have to have their manuscripts reviewed by peers. Colleague surveillance is very strong in this domain, not only regarding publications but also research grants. W&O psychologists working in these organisations strongly identify with the subject. The profession is an important frame of reference. Professionals see each other regularly at national and international conferences.

The second domain is different. Here it is the psychologists who provide services like selection and training. This is also a group which identifies with the profession. But their position is much weaker. There is competition from others. The domain is less exclusive. One wants to defend the domain but it is difficult to do this adequately. The domain is broad and it is difficult to define the borders.

The third domain is even broader. They are the people who have been trained as professional psychologists, but take up positions which can also be filled by other professionals. For such positions it is seen to be an advantage to have been trained as a psychologist, but there is no exclusiveness and the domain is hardly defensible. In 1976 Stanton pointed out in an APA book on career opportunities that there will be limited employment opportunities in traditional jobs. He foresaw opportunities in personnel administration and human resource development. This also emerges from European studies.

Professionals working in this domain usually do not fit in with the traditional model. They do not occupy one position for a lifetime, such as physicians do, but pursue a career, which is a succession of positions. They are organisation and career orientated. It is possible to exclude this domain from W&O psychology but it make sense to include it for a number of reasons. Teaching W&O psychology is an important activity for the profession. At universities, teaching is usually tied to doing research. So even when graduates do not enter the second domain, it is attractive to train students in W&O psychology. Furthermore the third domain has all kinds of relationships with the second domain. There is substantial overlap. Professionals in this area use W&O psychology knowledge and may even promote research.

Clients

Many psychologists will associate the word "client" with the code of conduct. Applicants taking part in a psychological test procedure are for psychologists the clients. A professional psychologist has to seek clients who will pay for his/her services. In traditional professions the client issue is not so complicated. Professionals provide consulting hours in where clients can come to see them. The professional will send them a bill later. In W&O psychology only a small minority find themselves in this situation. The majority is employed by an organisation from whom they receive a salary. In those circum-stances they may deal with individuals but it is the organisation which pays for the services.

A basic fact that every personnel psychologist needs to appreciate, whether he is working in industry, in civil service, or in the armed forces, is that the broad administrative decisions which determine the conditions under which he is to work and even the question of whether he is to continue to work will be made not by him but by the administrative superiors. Some person or persons in the top levels of management will have the power to decide that there is to be a personnel selection programme and that psychological tests are to be used. Someone will obtain funds for the programme. Someone will decide how much time of job applicants is to be made available for testing, and how much testing can be done with employees already on the job. The psychologist may be consulted on all these points. He will certainly have a opportunity to express his opinions and offer his recommendations. But the general decisions on the matters of policy will not be his.

This dependence on others for the continuing support of his activities raises a new set of practical problems which the personnel psychologist must face. They are problems of salesmanship. A personnel programme necessarily includes a selling programme, to guaranrcc continuing acceptance of and support for the programme. It is of critical importance to sell the programme to those members of top man agement who have powers of life or death over the programme. It is not always the top management who makes the decisions. There are organisations where also others have influence on the decision making. An example can be found in universities, where programmes are discussed in councils, and where the university is often dependent upon government support. So there are several parties having an influence on the life and death of programmes.

Selling is not an entirely rational process. Codes of conduct have some rules obliging the psychologist to give a fair representation of his/her services and qualifications. But the client is free, and can basically decide about "life or death" of a programme. And the client does not always use rational arguments. To clients a very important consideration is if the psychologist feels in the first instance an interest in his needs. There may be concern that the professional is more involved in his own interests. Clients often expect to see signs that the professional is loyal to the client or a client organisation. So the relationship is certainly not a neutral one. Usually the professionals have to prove themselves to the client and persuade him that the services have added value.

Psychologists often want to use arguments showing that these activities contribute to the profit of the organisation. For example by using psychological tests the organisation can hire more qualified applicants and these will contribute towards higher effectiveness and higher profit. Psychologists employed by an organisation often strongly identify with the interests of that organisation; particularly those who have to sell the programmes do so. Organisations expect their managers and experts to look after the interests of the organisation. New members of that group when They enter the organisation are taught in the socialisation process similarly to do so.

At the end of the sixties, in the period of student revolts, this created tension. There were heated discussions about the position of workers and a rather hostile climate developed against employers. Political parties were for thc introduction of a form of participation and industrial democracy. Psychologists working for industrial organisations were often seen as "lackeys of management". Discussions developed as to whether such psychologists, as well as personnel officers, should not in the first place identify with the interests of the workers. Such discussions took off first in the universities and schools for professional training. This created quite some role conflict and role ambiguity.

In that period there were groups of psychologists working at universities who expressed their loyalty towards workers. They wanted to assist workers in their struggles with employers. This approach was not appreciated by most of their colleagues but did attract interest on the part of students. There were also psychologists who felt it might be better to work for the labour unions but who soon discovered that there were very few positions available in such organisations. Yet other psychologists, working for universities, chose to concentrate on issues which raised fewer discussions.

Interest in personal selection declined rapidly; new issues such as industrial democracy and participation attracted much attention. Where formerly the field was known as industrial psychology, the name "Work and Organisational Psychology" came into use. This was in line with the broadening of the domain and the substantial number of W&O psychologists taking up positions in non-industrial organisations. The changing political climate, the discussions in the universities and the changes in the profession certainly had an impact on the position of psychologists in industrial organisations.

While formerly they had identified with the management, they now dealt with complex situations. Role senders in the professional associations and in the universities expressed different expectations to those of management and workers councils. Decision-making processes about programmes of psychologists were more complex too.

This episode in the development of W&O psychology shows that the relationship with the client is influenced by ideological and political issues and that strong emotions might be involved. It is clearly more complex than as described by Thorndike in 1949. Selling a programme is not an entirely rational activity. In organisations there are always conflicting interests and service providers can be caught out because parties try to use the services of the service provider for their own interests. This is why law and codes of conduct are important, because through such laws a better balanced decision can be made, to recognise the different interests involved.

Within a profession choices are made and that there should be the presence of some kind of managerial system. To start with there wiil be a professional association with a board and various divisions. Board members can stimulate discussion, approve programmes, approach government organisations, etc.,. Universities train new professionals. There may be general outlines for training programmes, but it is in the way universities set up their programmes that they contribute to the shaping of the domain. Within the profession there is a continuous discussion on all kind of topics, evident from the president's yearly addresses, and articles written by members.

The profession should concentrate on enlarging the knowledge base before concentrating on serving clients. Psychological knowledge is highly valued in finding answers to problems within organisations and see clearly a place for professional psychologists in providing services to clients. Within a profession there are conflicting views all the time. In discussions one tries to convince others. Researchers stress that more resources should be allocated to research projects and feel that basic issues should be included more in training programmes. Service providers want more support from the professional association in order to improve their position towards clients and competing professionals. They want to have training programmes placing more attention on practical problems.

Within each profession there is usually a dominant faction -a group of professionals who have been successful in making their own views prevail. Their definition of the situation is accepted by the majority of professionals. Members of that faction are elected to key positions. They are members of the board of the association but can also be appointed as professors in teaching and research programmes.

In such positions they defend the views of thc dominant faction. Their views are accepted because the majority of those in the profession are of the opinion that this offers the best approach to satisfying the demands the profession has to meet. The views of the dominant faction are usually also more acceptable to parties outside the profession. such as the clients and the government. A dominant faction is not necessarily homogeneous. It can be a coalition of different interests. Psychologists needed to establish themselves in the universities, but met opposition from the philosophers who often occupied the chairs in psychology. A coalition was formed from experimental and applied psychologists. What brought them together was the mutual need to get established within the university. Schönpflug has doubts about the wisdom of this coalition.

Dominant coalitions are not always successful at staying in power. Due to internal and external changes the views of the dominant coalition can prove less adequate and show a lower survival value. Other factions may be able to take over the position, as happened in the late fifties and early sixties in some European countries. Dutch psychology was very much influenced by German psychology. The approach was directed at "understanding" and not on "prediction". holistic methods were used. After the Second World War, younger psychologists discovered how much progress had been made in the USA, particularly in the period between 1935-1955. A new generation of psychologists started eagerly to read American literature. Van Strien shows in a study how psychologists who became professors before 1960 mainly quoted German literature in their thesis. Those who became professors after 1960 quoted Anglo-Saxon literature.

The first generation of psychologists disappeared mainly during the fifties and early sixties. With a new generation came a new dominant faction. This new faction was not clientoricntated, but wanted in the first case to enlarge the knowledge base. "More research is needed". The change is understandable. The first generation had been highly successful in making psychology acceptable to the general public and selling the subject to clients. But the knowledge base of the discipline was not strong, and when a new generation advocated concentrating on enlarging that knowledge base, they easily prevailed. New appointments in universities were mainly psychologists who had demonstrated that they could do research.

In a changing environment the dominant faction can change once again. In the USA the number of practising psychologists, particularly clinical psychologists, has increased considerably, and one can see that, starting in the late seventies, all kind of struggles take place in the psychological association. Clinical psychologists and university psychologists have their own candidates for the president of the association. The APA has tried hard to set up programmes for both groups. Nevertheless the scientifically orientated psychologists have established a new association (APS). Processes within a professional association are of a political nature. There are views and interests which are defended by individuals and groups but the processes help the profession to accommodate new demands. Also professions operate in a turbulent environment. Clients, but also the government, place new demands and the profession has to find ways of answering them.

TRAINING

For the continuity of the profession one has to recruit members, and such new members have to be trained. They have to become familiar with the approaches and values of the profession. A training programme is not only a transfer of knowledge, it is also a socialising process. Trainers are also role models. They familiarise new members with the expectations had by colleagues, clients and other role senders. And in particular they familiarise the new members with how the profession defines problems and how problems are approached. New members learn about the domain, and how clients can be best served. Such training does not only take place in lecture rooms. There has to be a period where new members go out and work under the supervision of experienced professionals. Gradually new members become more autonomous and become full members, fulfilling their own roles.

Training is highly important to the profession. It not only offers continuity but it also safeguards the professional culture. Just as there is continuous debate in the profession on how problems should be defined and approached, there is also continuous discussion on training. Also here there are competing factions and a dominant faction. Professional associations usually have quite some influence on training programmes both formally and informally. It is often members of the dominant faction who hold key positions both in the university, as in the association. Presidents of the association are often professors. Many members of important committees in the association are employed by universities. Officers in the association are often involved in accreditation and evaluation of training programmes.

To W&O psychologists a training programme is in the first instance training in psychology. W&O psychology is a field of application and a specialisation. In The Netherlands Duijker developed a model for the psychology training programme which was widely adopted, and even today is recognised. According to this model training should start with basic subjects like social psychology and experimental psychology, followed by introduction into fields of application like clinical psychology and W&O psychology. After this one specializes either in a basic subject or in a certain field of application. This model proved acceptable to a wide group of professionals. So there is clearly a broad coalition supporting this model, yet nevertheless Duijker's model has never been fully implemented. There have always been groups who wanted it to be modified in some way. But the overall approach remains a highly appreciated one, and has been mentioned in discussions over the decades.

Psychologists are also involved in training programmes of other professionals, e.g. pedagogues, business administrators, economists, physicians. Graduates of such programmes often compete in the labour market with W&O psychologists. Psychologists have even initiated new training programmes (e.g. agoges, personnel managers). Nevertheless the W&O psychology programme continues to recruit large numbers of students and has been fairly stable over the past decades. However, the competition in the labour market urges educators to make up their mind about what they want to accomplish. If those who graduate do not find adequate employment this will provoke all kind of tensions and might lead eventually to outside intervention. As a result the willingness to support such programmes might become eroded.

ENOP, a network of European W&O professors, has set up a reference model for W&O training programmes. This model corresponds with Duijker's approach; it also starts with basic subjects and introductions, after which the specialisation in W&O psychology follows. It distinguishes three streams: personn%l psychology, organisational psychology, and work psychology. For each stream courses are specified and described including the literature which can be used for such courses. Before setting up this reference model a review was made of European training programmes, thus it is based on a better definition of the domain of W&O psychology. The model is a good base for accreditation of training programmes.

The ENOP reference model clearly elect for a psychology training programme. Students should first of all become familiar with psychology. Employers often state that they look for applicants who have been seen to have mastered a certain subject but who are also familiar with the setting wherein the knowledge can be applied. In university training programmes both aspects can be seen. The ENOP model gives priority to the subject of psychology. This is also clear from a study done by de Wolff & Shimmin. They held a survey among 24 European W&O professors. Their respondents were clearly attached to a psychological training programme. When, due to economising measures, programmes had to be reduced one tried to retain the psychology section, and reduce the orientation in other subjects and in the work setting. The general idea was that such orientation should take place after the completion of the university programme. Such an approach is contrary to the one followed in business administration programmes. There the emphasis is much more on orientation, instead of mastering a particular discipline. It appears that employers appreciate the psychologists's approach.

Professional Association

The position of the professional association has changed due to a number of developments. A first development has to do with psychology having become an established discipline. For W&O psychology, the establishment process was more or less completed during the sixties. For example it was in this period most Dutch universities established chairs in W&O psychology. Psychology, including W&O psychology had become a recognised discipline. So the focus changed from that of becoming recognised to other issues, having more to do with expansion. Such a new stage brings its own problems. Objectives are no longer so common and inspiring to all the members of the profession. Factions within the profession are more inclined to pursue their own interests.

Associations and activities are highly dependent upon volunteers. Members spend a lot of time on administrative activities and committee work. To employ staff is costly and increases the membership fee. This in turn might discourage professionals from becoming a member, or may lead to the discontinuation of membership. Several authors point out that professionals are dedicated people. But when the goals of the association become less inspiring the willingness to take part in such activities will decrease. There has been a clear shift seen in membership.

For a long time university psychologists were in the majority but during the past two decades the number of practising psychologists, particularly clinical and health psychologists has increased enormously. Goodstein reports that in the USA between 1976 and 1985 the percentage of psychologists working at universities decreased from 47 to 34. In the same period the number of psychologists working in health care increased from 37 to 46.5. Pion et al. present figures about psychology PhDs. In 1973 about 56% of the psychologists who were working full time were employed by colleges and universities. In 1991 their share had dropped to 38%. Howard et al. presents a table showing that in 1972 the number of Health Service Provider PhDs surpassed the number of Academic/Research Subfield PhDs. Since then the former has continued to grow rapidly while the latter has declined.

So there is on the one hand a change in the composition of the profession, but also on the other a clear shift in the kind of employment. In Europe the decrease has been even larger. Employment opportunities at universities are bleak; graduates have to look for employment elsewhere. The shift has had consequences for the associations. University staff, having a dominant position in APA, were confronted by clinical and health psychologists wanting to take over the dominant position. APA has as its objective the promotion of psychology as a science, as well as a profession. APA has made a great effort to support both the researchers, who want to advance psychology and to increase the knowledge base and to advance psychologists as health providers. Nevertheless a group of university psychologists have established a new association: The American Psychological Society. This did not however have an effect on the membership of APA, there was uninterrupted growth.

The struggle between academic psychologists and health providers puts the W&O psychologists in a special position. They now go more their own way. In the USA the Society for Industrial and Organisational Psychology has become an independent organisation. In Europe the European Association of Work and Organisational Psychologists was founded in 1981. This association has relationships with national divisions, but also has allowed individual membership. This organisation concentrates on organising conferences and promoting the exchange of information.

There is a substantial difference between the association in the USA and European associations. The APA is, in comparison with European associations, a very big one. It has a staff of over S00 and a budget of about 60 million dollars. European associations have a much more modest size. For example, in 1996 the Dutch Association, NIP had a staff of 25 and a budget of 3.6 million guilders. There is a federation of European associations, EFPPA but this federation does not have its own professional office. Associations mainly operate on a national level.

The APA having more critical mass can operate on a more professional level. One activity which receives much attention is the influencing of government decision making processes. Government is by far the most important financier of research programmes, directly or indirectly and is also a very important employer and in so doing, has enormous impact on the development of psychology. The APA monitors government programmes and mal~,es sure that government officials and politicians are made aware of what psychologists can contribute. When there are hearings in Congress the APA presents the psychologist's view.

A profession has its own definition of problems and attempts to make others to accept these definitions. By presenting carefully documented views to the government APA is defending the domain of psychologists. APA has been doing this for several years. In the beginning this was done by a separate organisation because some members were sceptical about lobbying. Now it is a regular activity and the viewpoints presented at hearings are regularly published in the American Psychologist and in the Psychological Monitor. An advantage of this openness is that psychologists are more accountable for their views. Other professions can endorse but also dispute them. It stimulates debate. This is that others claim that they are more qualified, or not only important for the profession but also for clients.

In Europe this type of debate is much more restricted; this is probably due to the smaller size of the associations. Another effort has been made by the American Psychological Society. This society set up a committee, chaired by Milton Hakel, which identified six areas of broad national concern: Productivity in the workplace, schooling and literacy, the ageing society, drug and alcohol abuse, health and violence in America. The committee invited societies to prepare specific research initiatives that would be presented to Congress and federal and other agencies. It wanted to define tangible problems in the real world, describe current knowledge and to identity key issues that needed to be investigated. Also this is an example of where psychologists get involved in discussions on social problems and where they try to contribute to the solution of such problems. Other tasks for associations are the accreditation of training programmes and licensing. Where there is substantial economising, training programmes are threatened. It is important that quality is monitored, to make sure that the graduates meet standards set for good practice and research. one can feel more qualified oneself.

In the course of time there have been marked shifts. Until the sixties it seemed that sociologists would acquire a very strong position. At that time sociology was popular with students but later on the interest decreased. Nowadays business administration graduates (MBA) comprise the most important competitors. Business administration was enormously popular during the eighties and early nineties, while numbers are decreasing in the second half of the nineties, yet the study remains still quite popular. Competition also exists in other areas. For example selection services nowadays are provided by head-hunters and mediators who often offer packages of selection and recruitment. Those who offer such services are often non-psychologists. These developments show that positions can change considerably. Professions despite having a strong position can lose this in the course of time and neweomers can capture a substantial part of the market.

Relationship with Other Disciplines

Other professionals offer services or apply for positions and compete with W&O psychologists. The domain is not exclusive. Sometimes psychologists cooperate with other professionals, e.g. psychologists and sociologists working together as organisational consultants. But there is also direct competition, e.g. when different professionals apply for the same position. The relationship with other disciplines is ambivalent. Sometimes one feels that through cooperation one can offer better services. One will also experience

The government has much influence on the profession. This is partly because the government is a big employer and also, through funding, indirectly has much influence of employment but also regulates society through laws and programmes. When the government drafts laws and sets up programmes it has its own definition of problems. Such definitions can be in agreement with the views of psychologists but can also be very dificrent. Governments strive to stimulate employment to prevent discrimination and to improve health. They are constantly busy developing programmes. How such programmes are shaped is very much dependent on the perception it has on causes. If one feels that health problems are caused by stress, one looks for another means to solve the problem than when one feels problems are created by inadequate food or poor sanitation.

In western democracies there is a continuous debate about what government should do to improve a situation. There are always competing views and parties who try to influence the government. For the profession there are two kind of problems. One is government can develop programmes which interfere with the services provided by the profession. The other kind of problem has to do with knowledge which is available and is relevant for the government programmes.

There are a number of examples where government programmes interfered with services provided by W&O psychologists. In the fifties and sixties W&O psychologists constructed biographical inventories for personnel selection. They tried to find items which discriminate between applicants performing well and those performing poorly.

Their interest in the actual contents of the items was very limited. The real interest was in prediction. But the applicants had gained a different impression, and complained about the contents of the items. They felt that psychologists had not respected their privacy by asking questions about issues which were none of their business. Eventually the Congress organised hearings. It is still interesting to read about the discussions which developed, and to see how psychologists were forced to rethink the issue and to change their mind.

The government intervention started a discussion in the profession and psychologists had to redefine their definition of the problem. Similarly, the government's interventions to prevent discrimination forced psychologists to rethink their selection approaches. Government interventions can force professions to review their definitions of problems. It is striking that psychologists appeared often surprised by such interventions. They thought they were dealing with a psychological and scientific issue and were insufficiently aware of the political nature of such issues. It is also likely that in the future there will be interventions.

Since the domain has become so broad the chances of confrontations appear to be greater. The other issue has to do with the relevant knowledge. Setting up programmes is usually preceded by discussions in parliament and in the press. This is a period in which individuals and interest groups present their views and try to influence the decision-making processes. It is also a period in which governments consult experts and councils. It is during these interaction processes that programmes are shaped and where governments seek support for the programmes in order to minimise conflicts. Psychological research turns up new knowledge which often might be very useful for setting up programmes. Often such knowledge is brought to the attention of the government through councils and experts. There are issues however where, either through insufficient research or inadequate use of existing knowledge, programmes prove inadequate.

Service-Learning of Psychologists

Like many areas of applied psychology, the field of industrial/organisational psychology (I/O) also embraces the scientist-practitioner model. Yet, the training that is often provided by I/O graduate programs, especially those at the Ph.D. level, focus mainly on building students' scientist competencies. Yet, less than 40% of psychologists trained in I/O pursue an academic track where these competencies are most visible and valued. In addition, graduate programs in I/O do not formally train students to be practitioners. Students acquire sporadic and informal experience as practitioners through contract work and through assisting their faculty with their consulting. Rarely is there a formal mechanism whereby students work with faculty to understand the practitioner identity and the role of I/O practice for business and for society.

Service-learning (SL) appears to be an optimal vehicle for training students in I/O. SL offers students the opportunities to test out and develop their practitioner skills, but it also affords students the opportunity to learn about and embrace the values of I/O psychology. For example many I/O practitioners work in the area of organisation development, and the values and process of SL overlap considerably with those of OD. Specifically, Thomas & Landau discuss the congruence between OD and SL's values for reciprocal learning, reflection, collaboration, and empowerment.

Furthermore, the Society for I/O Psychology (SIOP) promotes collaboration between scientists and practitioners in order to continue the development of both the science and the practice of I/O, while simultaneously closing the gap between the two. Recent articles in *The Industrial/Organisational Psychologist* have also focused on the importance of pro bono work by I/O psychologists to the larger community as well as to the profession itself.

Through SL opportunities students not only enhance their chances of developing socially responsible knowledge, but they also gain the experience of collaborating with I/O professionals who are faculty members or practitioners. Together they can provide valuable services to those small business or community agencies that may not otherwise have the time, personnel, or financial resources to address needs that can be fulfilled by SL students.

In many ways SL is an ideal vehicle with which to train applied psychologists, especially those interested in I/O. Students working in a SL paradigm are able to acquire valuable experience while integrating that experience with traditional classroom instruction. Furthermore, SL helps to bridge the practitioner-scientist gap by making practitioners and other organisational members partners in learning. For students considering consulting careers, SL experiences help them assess their readiness for practitioner life and better discover the types of work environment in which they would like to practice. For students considering an academic career path, SL experiences provide them with the opportunities to enrich their instruction with real life experiences outside of academe. SL experiences, especially those that involve more community-oriented engagement, help students to better understand the vast opportunities for applying their knowledge, skills, and abilities.

Organisational Consulting Psychology

Organisational consulting psychologists work at multiple levels: directly with individuals, as with executive coaching, with dysfunctional or functional groups, or with the organisational system as a whole. However, fundamentally organisations are composed of individuals. This section identifies individual-level variables that we feel organisational consulting psychologists should understand. These variables are disucsse in two sets: traits rooted in the structure of personality, and presumably with a relatively larger influence from biological or even genetic factors, and those that appear to have a relatively larger cultural component and are aspects of character. In practice, it is difficult to draw a firm dividing line between these sets of variables. Even so, it is useful for the consulting psychologist to conceptualise a distinction between these two groups of variables, because traits are more difficult to modify, while character may-with effective interventions or policies-change or be changed, at least in its behavioural expressions.

Individual Traits

Over a century of research on differential psychology has focused on four domains of traits that are relevant for vocational and organisational selection: interests, abilities, personality, and features of psychopathology not already part of these domains. Ability traits have been shown to determine whether one can do something, personality traits the manner of how one does something, and interest traits the degree to which one is drawn or naturally motivated to do something. Abilities refer to performance, dimensions of personality to style, and interests to motivation. We shall address the first three areas; those interested in the nature of psychopathology and how it affects work adjustment can refer to Lowman.

Much of what we know about the dimensions of individual difference traits derives from factor analytic methods. Our reliance on factor analysis and related methods to identify traits is to some degree ironic and has some limitations. The irony is that the methods to identify psychological variables presumed to be important for specific individuals depend on identifying what is in common across individuals. This is not paradoxical, however, since individual uniqueness derives from the idiosyncratic combinations of sets of variables at the individual level that collectively define who a person is. Such variables may also be relevant to organisational behaviour and vocational adjustment, but it is difficult for an organisational consulting psychologist to identify them except through careful assessment or finely tuned clinical sensitivities. Other limitations of the methods arise from their inability to identify their relations to, say, biological or social causes. The methods are correlational and simply identify variables that hang together. Also, overly zealous advocates of the methods assume that broad factors identified through the methods are necessarily the most important and represent all the important variables in a domain. Neither is necessarily the case. It may be that particular facets of a broad factor are, in some applied contexts, more important to know and work with than the broad factor itself. Additionally, some important variables may be relatively rare but still important, and factor analytic methods will generally miss these.

Characteristics of individuals also exist that are more likely to mature given particular cross-domain or iterative combinations of primary characteristics. Such characteristics also develop only through interaction with, and through acquiring ideas provided by, the groups, organisations, and the wider culture in which the individual matures. Examples include identity, leadership, creativity, entrepreneurial character, and values. Many of these variables may function as memes, that is, as "elements of a culture that may be considered to be passed on by non-genetic means, especially imitation". A term originally coined by Dawkins, memes serve, within individuals, as the means of storage, replication, and transfer of complexes of ideas active at the cultural level. They act as a bridge between the individual, group, and organisation.

Of course, one might argue that memes constitute an interaction of two ability factors-crystallised intelligence and memory-but advocates of meme theory might argue that memes merely exploit such ability and other resources as a means of replicating themselves across individuals. For example, memes that direct individuals to act in creative ways might be more likely to copy into individuals with particular personality traits (high on openness, and high on the facets of aesthetics, ideas, and fantasy) and interests (artistic). Once incorporated by the individual, a creativity-related meme might serve to maximise behaviours that make use of particular abilities, which would in turn increase the likelihood of the meme's transmission to others. With those cautions in mind, we will briefly outline the characteristics of traits identified through research. Readers interested in a systematic treatment beyond this discussion can consult Lowman.

Interests

Interests refer to individual differences that govern the degree to which one feels that one must do something. Interests therefore relate to the element of motivation (or perhaps compulsion) regarding approach-avoidance behaviour. Strong, one of the pioneers of the measurement of interests, stated that they direct us toward "activities for which we have liking or disliking and which we go toward or away from, or concerning which we at least continue or discontinue the status quo; furthermore, they may or may not be preferred to other interests and they may continue varying over time. Or an interest may be defined as a liking/disliking state of mind accompanying the doing of an activity, or the thought of performing the activity". Interests do not require conscious thought; Strong said, "they remind me of tropisms. We go toward liked activities, go away from disliked activities".

Holland extended earlier findings of basic factors of interests into a very popular theory of six main personal orientations, or interest structures. Some authors have challenged the criticality of the six factors, and suggest instead that the number of factors is essentially arbitrary, or that there might exist more important underlying, second-order, or meta-factors. However, the six factors persist both in the research literature and in most popular treatments.

Our present concern is therefore with the six personal orientations that focus on interests, and not with his subsequently proposed vocational personality types, which are superordinate constructs that subsume interests as well as abilities, temperaments, values, and other variables. However, we shall refer to the six orientations by the same terms used for vocational personality types: Realistic, Investigative, Artistic, Social, Enterprising, and Conventional. They are discussed below.

— *Realistic interests* lead people to engage in mechanical activities, which extend to technical, hands-on, and outdoor activities that somehow involve mechanical operations, broadly considered. The essential question driving this interest pattern is: how can one manipulate the physical world to make things happen? Realistic interests are satisfied through opportunities to build, to manipulate objects, and to improve or work within the physical world.

— *Investigative interests* lead people to be motivated by and to engage in scientific activities, which include research, mathematics, and related development of novel products. The essential question driving Investigative interests is: why are things (or people) the way they are and how does one know that the answer is correct? Investigative interests are satisfied by opportunities to understand and call for analytical abilities.

— *Artistic interests* lead people to engage in creative activities across a wide range of specific content areas. They include the creation of works of art (visual, musical, literary, or dramatic) and related applications. The essential question driving Artistic interests is: how can one create something beautiful that has never before existed and bring it to the attention of others? Artistic interests are satisfied by opportunities to create.

— *Social interests* motivate people to be involved in people-oriented activities, such as those that may involve teaching, ministering, and especially helping others who are in difficulty. Essentially, Social interests promote behaviour that holds the promise of providing the satisfaction that comes with assisting others. The essential question driving Social interests is: how can one help reduce human suffering, regardless of its cause? Social interests are satisfied by opportunities to help, to be involved with people, and to engage others constructively.

— *Enterprising interests* influence people to enjoy and seek out leadership or persuasive roles, and to engage in activities that involve taking charge of groups, setting ambitious goals and persuading others to achieve them. Activities that involve adventure, striving, and clear and measurable outcomes are particularly interesting. The essential question driving Enterprising interests is: how can one realise important ambitions through bringing into alignment the energies of others? Enterprising interests are satisfied by opportunities to influence, persuade, and manage.

— *Conventional interests,* the final of the six patterns, direct people toward activities that involve precise, meticulous, and methodical activities. Such work often involves mathematical or computational tasks, the goal being to create a program or system that, used many times, promotes productive efficiency. The essential question driving Conventional interests is: what are the abstracted requirements of a situation that, properly understood and acted upon, most effi-ciently reach goals? Conventional interests are satisfied by opportunities to save.

Holland's interest model is far more sophisticated than the identification of six factors of interests. His carefully researched model looks at a variety of constructs such as interest factor groupings, employment census, and techniques for judging the degree of fit between a person's interest patterns and the work or avocational environment.

Abilities

Abilities are individual difference characteristics that affect how well one can do something; they predict quality and level of maximal performance. More specifically, abilities sequence and organise thoughts and other abilities to produce behaviours that lead to the effective completion of desired tasks. Because abilities may speak to what is possible and what potentially obstructs progress toward goal achievement, individuals who wish to believe that only personal will and motivation restrain advancement understandably can find the concept of abilities limiting. Out of this concern, among other sources, has emerged a promising literature on skill acquisition that seeks to deconstruct complex achievements into a series of more delimited competencies that can be analysed and presumably taught. Ericsson, among others, has demonstrated this approach to be an alternative at least to the notion of abilities as fixed and delimiting.

Nonetheless, the field of psychology is not yet ready to abandon the construct of abilities. Indeed, psychologists for many decades have sought to discover a reasonably small number of core abilities that appear to support learning and performance across a wide variety of activities. This has led to a debate as to whether abilities arise due to either underlying aptitudes or achievements. If abilities arise from aptitudes, then there exists a set of underlying (and presumably cognitive) abilities that affect learning ability. If abilities arise from achievements, then they are limited directly by practice, and ultimately by interests (motivation).

Regardless of their ultimate origin, research has identified several basic abilities that are of interest to the consulting psychologist. Carroll reviewed the literature on cognitive or intellectual abilities, and, following a reanalysis of a large number of datasets, proposed a structure of such abilities that has proven broadly influential, particularly among those responsible for developing intelligence and ability tests. Although this model largely derived from academic research and has yet to be applied widely to industrial or consulting applications, the model is useful and suggestive. Carroll proposed a three-stratum, hierarchical model of the structure of abilities, with narrow abilities, that is, those that affect a small number of real-life performances at stratum I, broader abilities at stratum II, and general cognitive ability, or g, perhaps the most influential of all abilities, at stratum III. The following discussion draws heavily from an adaptation of Carroll's theory by McGrew and Flanagan, who sought to integrate Carroll's theory with those of Cattell and Horn.

Intelligence and g: General intelligence (popularly called IQ) remains one of, if not the, most important individual difference variables in psychology. It is "a very general mental capability that, among other things, involves the ability to reason, plan, solve problems, think abstractly, comprehend complex ideas, learn quickly, and learn from experience". More than any other single measurable human trait, it predicts important outcomes in the areas of education, work, and general life experience.

Intelligence is so important because of the critical importance to a variety of occupational performances of reasoning and decision-making. It becomes even more critical as the settings in which work behaviour occurs become more complex, as they are in almost every area of modern life.

Intelligence is important but is not the only ability that matters in organisational consulting contexts. One problem is how to distinguish intelligence from other abilities, and whether such other abilities in some sense also constitute intelligences. Researchers usually operationalise intelligence as consisting of psychometric g, following Spearman's distinction between g and specific abilities. Some researchers then define non-g, specific abilities, as the variance associated with ability tests once the g variance has been removed. Other researchers, such as Carroll, Cattell, and Horn, instead consider specific abilities as facets that are admixtures of g and non-g specific abilities.

Fluid Intelligence (Reasoning): This ability helps people reason through problems requiring concentrated attention and careful reasoning of a logical nature. The ability benefits individuals performing novel tasks that cannot be performed automatically; essentially, the individual must create a mental representation of the set of variables or concepts important for completion of the task, and then initiate a set of steps required to successfully perform the task, presumably relying on this mental model in doing so.

This ability includes both major approaches to reasoning (inductive and deductive), drawing inferences and considering implications (and making extrapolations), thinking about concepts, and recognising relationships between elements of problems (and then solving the problems). This ability is broadly important in many work settings, particularly when the worker cannot rely on tried-and-true routines and established skills to get the job done. Organisational consulting psychologists must be high in this ability to succeed, because they constantly confront novel problems that often depend on understanding the relations of many factors for their solution.

Crystallised Intelligence (Knowledge): This ability refers to an individual's deep, broad knowledge of a culture and its effective application. In addition to helping people win on televised trivia game shows, this ability provides the raw information materials that support the successful application of more complex behaviours. For example, knowledge enhances leadership and creativity. Four facets of crystallised intelligence might be especially important in helping individuals contribute and adjust to organisations. They are:

— business knowledge,

— psychological knowledge,

— autobiographical knowledge, and

— biographical knowledge.

That business knowledge is important in business success almost goes without saying. Psychological knowledge, too, aids individuals in both collaborating and competing to attain goals. Autobiographical knowledge helps individuals recall both past actions that worked and those that did not. Finally, biographical knowledge helps individuals do the same through the study of others' lives; one sees this form of knowledge even in the memorisation of famous quotations by famous innovators and leaders, a penchant of many business executives. Biographical knowledge is especially important in the creation of paragons, in which one closely studies the biographies of individuals whose characteristics one seeks to emulate through one's own vocational behaviour. The consultant may be wise to gain an understanding of the set of paragons that individuals have created, for they serve as important resources guiding individual behaviour.

Memory, Short- and Long-Term: Although Carroll separates memory processes into short- and long-term broad factors, we combine them for the present discussion, because his shortterm factor includes only two facets, memory span and learning abilities, of which only the first is well understood, with the second facet also being associated with the long-term memory factor.

Short-term memory is a limitedcapacity system; individuals can hold only about seven (plus or minus two) units of information at a time. The ability involves retaining information in immediate awareness for use within a few seconds; an example of its use is remembering phone numbers. People use this ability hundreds of times a day without (generally) realising it, and any relative deficits can prove irksome, and may require close attention to information and the development of compensatory strategies, such as immediately writing new information down.

Long-term memory, also called long-term storage and retrieval, represents a set of abilities that collectively are like having a good librarian in your mind; the librarian effectively indexes (encodes) information when initially received, stores it in the proper place (long-term memory), and then can help you easily find it when needed (retrieval). Extending the metaphor, the ability does not depend on the size of the library (crystallised or quantitative intelligence), but rather the quality of the librarian. Closely related to this ability might be ideational or associational fluency, likely to be important to creativity.

In addition to the facets of memory discussed by Carroll and McGrew and Flanagan, there are two facets of memory that might be important for individuals in organisations but which are not yet well studied in that context: name-face matching, and interpersonal process recall. Some individuals are relatively better at learning associations between names and faces, which provides an advantage in many types of tasks and settings. Interpersonal process recall refers to the ability to encode and recall the process of interactions between individuals, including one's own thoughts and affective states. This is an ability that many counselors and psychologists excel at, but that will also aid managers working through others.

Quantitative Knowledge: This ability helps one solve math problems correctly. It involves the individual's store of acquired quantitative declarative knowledge (the rules) and procedural knowledge (how to apply the rules in practice). Many jobs require substantial quantitative knowledge.

Visual (Spatial) Processing: This ability subsumes the variety of narrow abilities that relate to thinking about visual images, including the facets of the generation, storage, retrieval, and transformation of images. Individuals high in this ability might be more likely to think in terms of images rather than, say, words, and can manipulate shapes visually as might be needed by architects, engineers, and electricians. Such individuals might be more likely to draw pictures (or doodle) to represent their thoughts than to put them into words, serving also as an aid to spur further visual thinking. Without some visual imagery to focus and hold their thoughts, individuals high in this ability may be prone to losing their attentional focus. We suggest two facets of this ability that relate to social skills: reading facial affect and reading body language. Both can facilitate responsiveness in social interaction and the reception of emotional cues beyond those conveyed by communication through speech.

Auditory Processing: This ability depends on sound and our sense of hearing. Its exercise involves the production, storage, retrieval, and transformation of sounds. Individuals high in this ability will generally find it easy to acquire and remember information obtained through hearing. We suggest one additional facet of this ability, perceive affect in voices, that enhances the quality of communication through speech.

Reading/Writing: This ability is not well-defined or researched in the context of broad arrays of abilities, but appears to subsume a number of very narrow component abilities (for example, reading, decoding, and spelling) that, at more complex levels, support such activities as comprehending written passages and writing stories. As with quantitative knowledge, this ability includes both declarative and procedural aspects. Lack of ability in this area can impose steep limitations on advancement through many careers, and some research suggests that an alarmingly high proportion of the American public possesses levels of literacy that are marginal.

Processing Speed: This is the first of two broad speed abilities, and refers to mental quickness and performing cognitive tasks automatically and efficiently in ways that make minimal demands on mental capacity, especially important when an individual must focus attention and concentration. Processing speed does not refer to simple reactions, but rather to sustaining an efficient and rapid mental process over some duration.

Decision/Reaction Time or Speed: This second broad speed ability relates to an individual's quickness in making decisions or reacting quickly. It facilitates the speediness of immediate reactions.

Clearly, it will rarely be possible or even desirable to measure all abilities in a particular organisational consulting application. Still, this review of job-relevant abilities implies that it would be very naïve to assume that a single ability trait, even one as broad as intelligence, would be universally applicable. As importantly, occupations, and therefore organisations, are not created tabula rasa. When theories are proposed of such sweeping concepts as organisational learning, it should not be forgotten that organisations, among other things, are the sum (or is it multiplier?) of their individual ability patterns. Some organisations select for and retain only the highest end of the ability spectrum; for others, abilities are less important and the array of talent is more limiting. Such individual difference variables are rarely considered when measuring organisational-level variables that might de facto be influenced by the ability constellation of employees.

Personality Traits

Personality traits refer to the way people view the world and the manner and style in which they do things, and therefore predict the style as well as the content of behaviour. Although some early theorists and researchers discussed the importance of this domain for education, work, and everyday life, most of the discussion of personality was, until the last few decades, primarily focused on psychopathology.

Hogan and Roberts credit the rising importance of personality psychology within organisational psychology to several causes. First, the use of cognitive ability testing may result in adverse impact for some protected classes of job seekers under U.S. law, while well-constructed measures of personality generally do not. Second, the rise of factor-analytically based taxonomies of personality-and especially the fivefactor model-provided a way to organise thousands of different personality measures within a handful of broad groups of traits, which helped to rationalise an otherwise unwieldy literature. Third, various content- and meta-analytic reviews of the literature on personnel and selection demonstrated the important roles that personality traits could play in the prediction of job performance and adjustment. Thus, personality traits, like abilities, predict important work and organisational outcomes, and, like abilities, one may classify them into one of a few broad categories.

A major question in discussing the personality variables relevant for organisational consulting psychology is whether one need only focus on the big five personality traits, or whether focus should also extend to the facets, or components, of the big five, and perhaps to other traits as well. Paunonen and Nicol argue that in many practical applications, one can obtain greater benefits from using the facets instead of focusing only on the broad, overarching factors.

However, there is no universally agreed on list of these facets, to parallel the consensus on the big five factors; different authors have proposed different sets (or at least names) of these facets and narrow personality traits. For example, Lowman describes the organisational importance of such additional personality traits, including achievement orientation, need for power, and masculinity-femininity. Our present discussion of the big five traits and their facets draws from that used in the Revised NEO Personality Inventory.

Although both the measure and its ability to measure facets are not without criticism, Piedmont favorably reviews the empirical support for both the general domain and facet scales, also citing Costa and McCrae's discussion of the conceptual relations of the domains and their facets. Tinsley speculated that the personality factor and facet scores of the NEO-PI might overlap with some of the personality and adjustment constructs thought to be important to work adjustment. However, we are mindful that just because the authors of the NEO-PI-R report the existence of a particular facet does not necessarily mean that the facet is viewed as critical for organisational behaviour, or that there exists any degree of consensus around its practical usefulness. Therefore, we will note which of these facets have received the most empirical support in organisational research.

Conscientiousness. This might be the most important of the big five traits in terms of impact on work performance and adjustment to organisations. Costa and McCrae report that important facets include competence, order, dutifulness, achievement striving, selfdiscipline, and deliberation, all characteristics that managers generally value in their employees. Dutifulness is an important construct in the study of organisational issues related to military personnel.

Extraversion/Introversion. Many authors also describe this trait as being important to organisational adjustment, and for the prediction of job tenure and for influencing how one tries to accomplish work. Costa and McCrae report that facets include warmth, gregariousness, assertiveness, activity, excitement seeking, and positive emotions. Many organisational theorists and researchers refer to the constructs warmth, gregariousness, assertiveness, activity, excitement-seeking, and positive emotions. Extraversion/introversion describes personality variables of temperament that reflect not so much social gregariousness as need for time to oneself and seeking stimulation internally versus externally.

Agreeableness: Although the evidence for its prediction of work-related outcomes is limited except for jobs involving interpersonal interactions, the personality trait of agreeableness is included in most big five models of personality. Individuals high in this trait are easy to get along with and trust, while individuals low in the trait leave others on edge and wary of direct contact. Researchers and scientists typically are low on the trait, and may express the trait through skepticism and lack of faith that something is so just because someone says so.

There are many other ways to express disagreeableness, just as there are many types of vinegar. Organisational consulting psychologists may encounter this trait (on the low, disagreeable end) through individuals who, for a variety of reasons, seem to have a hard time fitting in. However, individuals at the high end of the trait may, depending on the demands of their role and position, also face difficulties. For example, executives of charitable foundations that give grants find themselves being asked repeatedly for money and faith; if the executive is too agreeable, and cannot learn to say no without regret, he or she will experience enormous stress and ultimately fail. According to Costa and McCrae, facets of the trait include trust, straightforwardness, altruism, compliance, modesty, and tender-mindedness. Most of these constructs have been of interest to organisational researchers, including trust, straightforwardness, altruism, compliance, and modesty.

Openness to Experience. This trait also has had mixed results in predicting occupational outcomes, and appears to be a complex trait. Presumably, the trait's importance will vary in importance depending on the nature of the organisation's or work unit's mission. It may also predict more to career choice than to occupational performance issues.

Individuals low on the trait would be expected to be more likely to focus on the practical side and to eschew imagination; this can be very useful when the purpose of the organisation is to focus on unexciting details and just get the job done. On the other hand, in organisations that require flexibility of response and must foster independent and creative problem solving, individuals high on the trait can prove very important.

An interesting aspect of this trait is that it seems to be positively correlated to measures of intelligence (g). Costa and McCrae describe the facets of this trait as fantasy, aesthetics, feelings, actions, ideas, and values. Although organisational researchers and theorists have explored issues related to many of these facets at an abstract or organisational level, or perhaps in terms of characteristics of the leaders of organisations (especially in relation to factors that support charismatic or transformative leadership), the facets (as traits) seem not to have been heavily researched among the general membership of organisations.

Neuroticism. Neuroticism, along with extraversion/introversion, was one of the earliest of the broad personality traits identified by researchers. People on the high end of the trait tend to be anxious, become depressed, have poor self-concept, and experience negative emotions. Work can be adversely affected by neuroticism except, to some extent, in certain creative occupations in which neuroticism may be both expected and, within limits, even enhance performance. Facets reported by Costa and McCrae include anxiety, angry hostility, depression, selfconsciousness, impulsiveness, and vulnerability. Anxiety and self-consciousness have served as a focus in organisational research. Although angry hostility per se has not received attention from organisational researchers, workplace violence and its causes certainly have, along with personality correlates of other hostile workplace behaviour. Depression has been researched extensively in organisational contexts, although apparently not as a dispositional style. Finally, impulsiveness seems to have received little attention from organisational consultants except as a feature of various disorders, such as narcissism. Judge and Bono argue that neuroticism should be conceptualised even more broadly, also incorporating emotional stability and negative emotionality, along with other tendencies related to core self-evaluation, such as self-esteem, generalised self-efficacy, and locus of control.

Other Personality Issues: An unresolved question in the study of personality traits is the degree to which they rest on underlying temperaments, presumed to be present from birth. Strelau provides an excellent review of this literature, essentially concluding that although there may be some evidence that each of the big five broad personality traits may rest to some degree on underlying temperamental variables, the strongest evidence points to just two areas of personality: extraversion and neuroticism.

Because these traits have relatively strong linkages to underlying, physiologically determined temperaments, they might be especially resistant to modification in adulthood. Of course, any worker might act the part for a while, but perhaps especially in these traits, individuals will revert to temperamental type over time. Readers interested in learning more about the role of personality in organisations are directed to Lowman and Roberts and Hogan.

As with occupational interests, complex patterns are as important as measuring individual variables. Configurations of personality traits and their patterns in relationships to particular organisational variables might help moderate the impact of single dimensions of personality. Similarly, most personality traits are not linear in their influence on work outcomes: too much aggressiveness might, depending on the job, organisation, or culture, be as problematic as too little.

If patterns of variables are important within a single domain, they are even more important-but far less studied-across domains. Pioneering work in examining, at the individual-level analysis, interdomain relationships has been offered by certain researchers. Much more research is needed before conclusions can reliably be drawn about the effects of interests, personality, and ability as they interact with each other. However, as new studies emerge, in time it will be possible to understand the nuances of interdomain relationships that, it would be expected, sometimes compensate for areas of relative weakness, or that sometimes may add constraints.

References

Tompkins, Jonathan R. (2005) *Organization Theory and Public Management*. Thompson Wadsworth.

Kanigel, R. (1997). *The One Best Way, Frederick Winslow Taylor and the Enigma of Efficiency.* London: Brown and Co.

Simon, Herbert A. (1997)*Administrative Behavior: A Study of Decision-Making Processes in Administrative Organizations,* 4th ed., The Free Press.

Bibliography

Amabile, T. M. (1983). The social psychology of creativity: A componential conceptualization. *Journal of Personality and Social Psychology,* 45, 357-376.

Anderson, N., et.al., (eds.) (2002). *Handbook of industrial, work and organizational psychology, Volume 2: Organizational psychology.* Thousand Oaks, CA: Sage Publications Ltd.

Anderson, N., Ones, D. S., Sinangil, H. K., & Viswesvaran, C. (Eds.). (2002). *Handbook of industrial, work and organizational psychology, Volume 1: Personnel psychology.* Thousand Oaks, CA: Sage Publications Ltd.

Ash, M.G. (1992). "Cultural Contexts and Scientific Change in Psychology: Kurt Lewin in Iowa." *American Psychologist*, Vol. 47, No. 2, pp. 198-207.

Borman, W. C., & Motowidlo, S. J. (1993). Expanding the criterion domain to include elements of contextual performance. Chapter in N. Schmitt and W. C. Borman (Eds.), *Personnel Selection.* San Francisco: Josey-Bass (pp. 71-98).

Borman, W. C., et.al., (eds.) (2003). *Handbook of psychology: Vol 12 Industrial and organizational psychology.* Hoboken, NJ: John Wiley & Sons.

Bureau of Labor Statistics, U.S. Department of Labor, *Occupational Outlook Handbook, 2008-09 Edition*, Psychologists.

Buss D.M. (Ed.), *The handbook of evolutionary psychology* (pp. 724–746). New York: Wiley.

Campbell, J. P., Gasser, M. B., & Oswald, F. L. (1996). The substantive nature of job performance variability. In K. R. Murphy (Ed.), *Individual differences and behavior in organizations* (pp. 258–299). San Francisco: Jossey-Bass.

Campbell, J.P. (1990). Modeling the performance prediction problem in industrial and organizational psychology. In M.D. Dunnette & L.M. Hough (Eds.), *Handbook of industrial and organizational psychology* (2nd ed., Vol 1, pp. 687-732). Palo Alto, CA: Consulting Psychologists Press.

Campbell, J.P. (1994). Alternative models of job performance and their implications for selection and classification. In M.G. Rumsey, C.B. Walker, & J.H. Harris (Eds.), *Personnel selection and classification* (pp. 33-51). Hillsdale, NJ: Erlbaum.

Copley, F. B. (1923). *Frederick W. Taylor father of scientific management, Vols. I and II.* New York: Taylor Society.

Di Martino, V. & Mohtar, M. (2001). *Guidance for the Prevention of Stress and Violence at the Workplace.* Kuala Lumpur: Department of Occupational Safety and Health Malaysia.

Du Toit, M. (2003) *IRT from SSI.* Mooresville, IN: Scientific Software.

Dunnette, M. D. (Ed.). (1976). *Handbook of industrial and organizational psychology*. Chicago: Rand McNally.

Dunnette, M. D., & Hough, L. M. (Eds.). (1991). *Handbook of industrial/ organizational psychology* (4 Volumes). Palo Alto, CA: Consulting Psychologists Press.

Everly, G. S., Jr. (1986). An introduction to occupational health psychology. In P. A. Keller & L. G. Ritt (Eds.), *Innovations in clinical practice: A source book, Vol. 5* (pp. 331-338). Sarasota, FL: Professional Resource Exchange.

Flanagan, J. C. (1954). The critical incident technique. *Psychological Bulletin, 51*, 327-358.

Geary, D.C. (1998). *Male, female: The evolution of human sex differences.* Washington, DC: APA Press.

Goldstone, R., Roberts, M., & Gureckis, T.(2008). Emergent processes of group behavior Group Behavior,17, 1-15.

Guion, R. M. (1998). *Assessment, measurement and prediction for personnel decisions*. Mahwah, NJ: Lawrence Erlbaum.

Hatch, M.J., (2006) *"Organization Theory: Modern, symbolic, and postmodern perspectives."* 2nd Ed. Oxford University Press

Hayduk, L.A. (1987). *Structural equations modeling with lisrel.* Baltimore, MD: Johns Hopkins University Press.

Hedges, L. V., & Olkin, I. (1984). Nonparametric estimators of effect size in meta-analysis. *Psychological Bulletin, 96*, 573-580.

Hersey, P. and K.H. Blanchard (1982) *Management of Organisational Behaviour; utilizing Human Resources.* 4th Edition. Prentice Hall of India Pvt. Ltd. New Delhi 110 001. P. 343.

Hunter, J. E. (1986). Cognitive ability, cognitive aptitude, job knowledge, and job performance. *Journal of Vocational Behavior, 29*, 340-362.

Hunter, J. E., & Schmidt, F. L. (1990). *Methods of meta-analysis: Correcting error and bias in research findings.* Newbury Park, CA: Sage.

Hunter, J.E., & Schmidt, F. L. (1994). Estimation of sampling error variance in the meta-analysis of correlations: Use of average correlation in the homogeneous case. *Journal of Applied Psychology, 79*, 171-177.

Hunter, J.E., Schmidt, F. L., & Pearlman, K. (1981). Task differences as moderators of aptitude test validity in selection: A red herring. *Journal of Applied Psychology, 66*, 166-185.

Jex, S. M., & Britt, T. W. (2008). *Organizational Psychology*. Hoboke, New Jersey: John Wiley & Sons, Inc.

Jones, Ishmael, (2008) *The Human Factor: Inside the CIA's Dysfunctional Intelligence Culture.* New York: Encounter Books.

Kanigel, R. (1997). *The One Best Way, Frederick Winslow Taylor and the Enigma of Efficiency.* London: Brown and Co.

Kolb, D.A., I.M.. Rubin and J.M. Mc Intyre (1979) *Organizational Psychology – an experiential approach.* Third edition Prentice-Hall, INC., Englewood cliffs, New Jersey 07632. P. 496.

Koppes, L. L. (Ed.). (2007). *Historical perspectives in industrial and organizational psychology*. Mahwah, NJ: Lawrence Erlbaum.

Kotter, John P. (1990). What Leaders Really Do. *Harvard Business Review, May-June, 103-111.*

Lant, T.K, "Organizational Cognition and Interpretation," in Baum, (Ed)., *The Blackwell Companion to Organizations*. Oxford: Blackwell Publishers.

Law, K. S., Schmidt, F. L., & Hunter, J. E. (1994). A test of two refinements in procedures for meta-analysis. *Journal of Applied Psychology, 79*, 978-986.

Lowman, R. L. (Ed.). (2002). *The California School of Organizational Studies handbook of organizational consulting psychology: A comprehensive guide to theory, skills and techniques.* San Francisco, CA: Jossey-Bass.

Maslach, C. (1998). Burnout. In J.M. Stellman (Ed.), *Encyclopaedia of Occupational Health and Safety* (pp. 34.64). Geneva: International Labour Office.

Michelson, B. J. (2001). *Leadership and power base development: using power effectively to manage diversity and job-related interdependence in complex organizations*. Retrieved from http://www.au.af.mil/au/awc/awcgate/au-24/michelson.pdf

Nunnally, J., & Bernstein, I. (1994). *Psychometric theory* (3rd ed.). New York: McGraw-Hill.

O'Driscoll, M. P., & Cooper, C. L. (1994). Coping with work-related stress: A critique of existing measures and proposal for an alternative methodology. *Journal of Occupational and Organizational Psychology, 67*, 343-354.

Organ, D.W. (1977). A reappraisal and reinterpretation of the satisfaction-causes-performance hypothesis. *Academy of Management Review*, 2, 46-53.

Organ, D.W. (1994). Organizational citizenship behavior and the good soldier. In M.G. Rumsey, C.B. Walker, & J.H. Harris (Eds.), P*ersonnel selection and classification* (pp. 53-67). Hillsdale, NJ: Erlbaum.

Raudenbush, S. W., & Bryk, A. S. (2001). *Hierarchical linear models: Applications and data analysis methods* (2nd ed.). Newbury Park, CA: Sage.

Robbins, Stephen P. (2004) *Organizational Behavior - Concepts, Controversies, Applications.* 4th Ed. Prentice Hall.

Rogelberg, S., G. (Ed.). (2002). *Handbook of research methods in industrial and organizational psychology.* Malden, MA: Blackwell.

Rosenthal, R. (1995). Writing meta-analytic reviews. *Psychological Bulletin, 118*, 183-192.

Rosenthal, R., & DiMatteo, M. R. (2002). Meta-analysis. In H. Pashler & J. Wixted (Eds.). *Stevens' handbook of experimental psychology (3rd ed.), Vol. 4: Methodology in experimental psychology*, pp. 391-428. Hoboken, NJ, US: Wiley.

Sackett, P. R., & Wilk, S. L. (1994). Within group norming and other forms of score adjustment in pre-employment testing. *American Psychologist, 49,* 929-954.

Schmidt, F. L., & Hunter, J. E. (1998). The validity and utility of selection methods in personnel psychology: Practical and theoretical implications of 85 years of research findings. *Psychological Bulletin, 124,* 262-274.

Schmidt, F. L., Law, K., Hunter, J. E., Rothstein, H. R., Pearlman, K., McDaniel, M. (1993). Refinements in validity generalization methods: Implications for the situational specificity hypothesis. *Journal of Applied Psychology, 78*, 3-12.

Scott, W. Richard. (2007) *Organizations and Organizing: Rational, Natural, and Open Systems Perspectives.* Pearson Prentice Hall.

Simon, Herbert A. (1997)*Administrative Behavior: A Study of Decision-Making Processes in Administrative Organizations,* 4th ed., The Free Press.

Tompkins, Jonathan R. (2005) *Organization Theory and Public Management*. Thompson Wadsworth.

Weick, Karl E. (1979)*The Social Psychology of Organizing* 2nd Ed. McGraw Hill.

Yukl, G., & Falbe, C. M. (1991). Importance of different power sources in downward and lateral relations. *Journal of Applied Psychology, 76*, 416-423.

Index